Medieval Philosophy

A Beginner's Guide

ONEWORLD BEGINNER'S GUIDES combine an original, inventive, and engaging approach with expert analysis on subjects ranging from art and history to religion and politics, and everything in between. Innovative and affordable, books in the series are perfect for anyone curious about the way the world works and the big ideas of our time.

SELECTED FORTHCOMING TITLES:

Medieval
Philosophy
A Beginner's Guide

Sharon M. Kaye

ONEWORLD

OXFORD

A Oneworld Book

Published by Oneworld Publications 2008

Copyright © Sharon M. Kaye 2008

ISBN 978-1-85168-578-3

Typeset by Jayvee, Trivandrum, India
Cover design by Simon McFadden
Printed and bound in the United States of America
by Thomson–Shore Inc.

Oneworld Publications
185 Banbury Road
Oxford OX2 7AR
England
www.oneworld-publications.com

Contents

Preface and Acknowledgments

Welcome to *Medieval Philosophy: A Beginner's Guide*. It grows from ten years of experience teaching an undergraduate medieval philosophy course. I developed this course with the conviction that the only way to appreciate the unique contribution of the middle ages is to read what the authors themselves actually wrote. This presents an immediate problem, however, because medieval writings are not accessible to the beginner. I have therefore carefully excerpted, translated, and edited all of the classic passages to be discussed in this book. In so doing, I hope to have preserved their central insights while eliminating unnecessary complications. At the end of the book there is a section for further reading where you will find reference to complete versions of the works along with useful secondary sources.

This book aims to present all the best ideas of the middle ages in a way that will enable you, the modern reader, to make a personal assessment of them. Many aspects of medieval philosophy are still with us, living in our minds and in our hearts. We investigate their origin in order to understand ourselves better.

I truly enjoyed writing this book. I would like to thank my students over the years for showing me which ideas are still important and why. I am grateful to John Carroll University for providing a generous research leave during the spring of 2006, when I conceived this project. My thanks go also to Martin

Tweedale, professor emeritus at the University of Alberta, as well as Marsha Filion and Mike Harpley at Oneworld for their helpful suggestions and encouragement. Finally, I would like to dedicate this book to my husband Tris – *Quos amor verus tenuit, tenebit.*

Sharon Kaye

Timeline of major authors

ANCIENT PERIOD
    SOCRATES   *c.* 470–399 BC
    PLATO   *c.* 427–347 BC
    ARISTOTLE   384–322 BC

MEDIEVAL PERIOD
    AUGUSTINE   AD 354–430
    BOETHIUS   *c.* 475– 526
    ANSELM   1033–1109
    ABELARD   1079–1142
    AVERROES   1126–1198
    MAIMONIDES   *c.* 1138–1204
    THOMAS AQUINAS   1225–1274
    PETER JOHN OLIVI   1248–1298
    JOHN DUNS SCOTUS   *c.* 1265–1308
    WILLIAM OF OCKHAM   *c.* 1285–1347

RENAISSANCE

Introduction

The medieval period, also known as the middle ages, spans roughly the years AD 400 to 1400. Since the printing press was not invented until 1440, intellectual culture was very different then from what we are used to today. Books were written and copied by hand on treated animal skins, making them extremely valuable and rare. It's hard to believe such a primitive society could possibly have anything to say to us in the twenty-first century.

Although we are far ahead of the medievals when it comes to technology, we aren't so far ahead when it comes to philosophy. Many of the philosophical ideas first proposed in the middle ages are still current among us. During the years between AD 400 and 1400 the Catholic Church came to dominate all of Europe. The main priority of those few who were fortunate enough to be educated was to try to make sense of religious doctrine and pass it on to the next generation. Hence, medieval philosophy is primarily concerned with deep questions raised by the existence of God. The ideas medieval philosophers developed to answer these questions have endured. Most people around the world today still believe in God. It is not surprising to find, therefore, that medieval discussions of the questions that the existence of God raises remain interesting and useful.

We trace the beginning of the middle ages to the year AD 400 because this date marks the end of Roman Empire. The Roman Empire was an advanced civilization established in the third century BC with a complex system of laws, infrastructure, and culture. At the height of its glory, it stretched across Europe, all the way from Britain to Asia Minor. Its collapse at the beginning of the fifth century led to several hundred years of chaos, including ongoing wars, famines, and plagues. The period from around 550 to around 1050 is often referred to as the 'dark ages' because it allowed for only a very limited amount of learning and development. Few people could even read or write. The Roman language, Latin, slowly transformed into the various Romance languages we know today (French, Portuguese, Spanish, Italian).

One of the most important features of the Roman Empire, which helped to make it so successful for so many years, was its assimilation of the Greek golden age. Just as the greatest Roman buildings were inspired by Greek architecture, the greatest Roman ideas were inspired by Greek philosophers. This pattern did not change after the fall of the Roman Empire. On the contrary, the scarcity of books and widespread fear of new ideas reinforced it. Medieval philosophers were deeply dependent on the works of the two greatest philosophers of ancient Greece, namely, Plato and Aristotle. Early on, they had no direct access to the works of Plato and Aristotle because they could not read Greek and there were no translations. Nevertheless, they learned about Plato and Aristotle indirectly and as time went on they gained access to translations.

Because medieval philosophy lasted a millennium and spanned the many different cultures of Europe, it is complex and worthy of detailed, in-depth study. Nevertheless, every study must begin somewhere, and at the beginning it is helpful to have a simple framework for understanding the big picture. Plato and Aristotle provide us with this framework. Because they advocated opposing philosophies they established two poles between which medieval authors can be located.

In this book, we will focus primarily on the three major medieval philosophers Augustine, Thomas Aquinas, and William of Ockham. Plato's approach is paramount in the early middle ages, as Augustine shows in his Christian neoplatonism.

SCHOLASTICISM c. 1100–1500

Even during the darkest part of the medieval period the Catholic Church needed schools for educating priests. Over time these schools gave rise to the university system we know today. The first universities, established around 1200, offered only three graduate degrees: medicine, law, or theology. Philosophy thrived within the faculty of theology.

The Church was concerned to show how religious faith could be reconciled with scientific reasoning. It therefore required theology students to examine statements from religion and science that appear to conflict and to show how the conflict could be resolved. The twelfth-century theologian Peter Lombard collected these statements into a book and called it *The Sentences*. Thereafter, every theology student was required to write a *Commentary on the Sentences*. This involved very detailed logical analysis and argumentation. The resulting dialectical method of learning came to be known as 'scholasticism.'

To Renaissance thinkers, who were trying to free themselves from the domination of religion, the scholastics seemed overly bookwormish. The term 'scholastic' has retained this negative connotation today.

By the high middle ages, we see a shift to moderate Aristotelianism, as exemplified in the work of Aquinas. Ockham serves primarily as a critic of both neoplatonism and moderate Aristotelianism, pushing toward an extreme interpretation of Aristotle. Intervening discussions of Boethius, Anselm, Abelard, Averroes, and Scotus, inter alia, will fill out our picture of the medieval period as a whole.

This book presents all the most compelling ideas of the medieval philosophers along with their method for thinking about them. We'll investigate intriguing questions that have probably occurred to you at one time or another, such as the following: Does God exist outside of time? How does God know the future? Is it possible to prove God exists? Why do bad things happen to good people? Am I free? Why be moral? Medieval philosophers developed classic answers to these questions that are still among the very best available.

In addition to the answers themselves, medieval philosophers also developed a powerful method for thinking about such questions, namely, logic. Stylistically, the most distinctive thing about medieval philosophy is its dense argumentation. Authors used recognizable logical patterns to prove their points and to challenge their opponents' theories. In true medieval style we will apply this rigour throughout our study.

1

The ancient legacy

> The unexamined life is not worth living.
>
> Socrates

Due to their divergent philosophies, Plato and Aristotle launched opposing ways of thinking about the world that were at odds throughout the middle ages. Although some philosophers maintained that the ideas of the two great ancient philosophers could ultimately be harmonised, there was no widespread agreement about how this could be accomplished. The conflict between Plato and Aristotle actually proved to be very fruitful, however, because it pushed each side to make the best arguments possible.

Argumentation is the way philosophy progresses and logic is the backbone of argumentation. In order to understand what our medieval authors were trying to accomplish we will need to be able to dissect the structure of their reasoning. We therefore begin this chapter with a survey of the basic principles of logic that Plato, Aristotle, and their successors bequeathed to the middle ages.

The Socratic method

The word 'logic' comes from the Greek word '*logos*' meaning reason. We use the same word at the end of our scientific disciplines, such as 'biology' and 'psychology' to mean 'the systematic study of —.' Logic is systematic study. It stipulates the rules of thought itself. Logic started in ancient Greece and became a sophisticated tool in the hands of medieval philosophers.

SOCRATES c. 470–399 BC

Socrates is known as the founder of Western philosophy.

Although Socrates was a sculptor by trade, he preferred to spend his time hanging around the public square in Athens and engaging passers-by in conversation. For example, Socrates might try to provoke a lawyer into a debate about the nature of justice. Because he was good at arguing and had a lot of interesting ideas, Socrates became known as a 'philosopher' from the Greek words for 'love of wisdom.' He attracted a following of fans.

Socrates also made a lot of enemies, however, by questioning authority and challenging the status quo. Eventually he was tried, convicted, and executed for impiety and corrupting the youth.

Socrates is the first on record to develop and employ a method of systematic study. It is called the 'elenchus,' meaning cross-examination. Although Socrates did not write any books, his student Plato wrote many books about him. Appropriately enough, the elenchus first appears in a work called *The Apology*, in which Plato describes a court trial at which Socrates had to defend his own reputation.

During the trial, Socrates announces that God revealed to him that he is the wisest among men. Admitting that he himself did not at first believe the revelation, he proceeds to show how, and in what sense, he learned it to be true.

MY DEFENCE

After long consideration, I finally thought of a method of testing the question. I reflected that if I could find someone wiser than myself, then I might go to God with a refutation in my hand. I would say to God: 'You said that I was the wisest, but here is someone who is wiser than I am!'

Accordingly, I went to a man who had a reputation for wisdom and the result was as follows: When I began to talk

with him, it became evident that his supposed 'wisdom'
consisted in the fact that he *thought* himself to be wise. When I
tried to explain that *thinking* you are wise is not the same as *being*
wise he grew to hate me. So I left him, saying to myself as I
went away: 'Well, even though neither of us is wise, I'm better
off than he is. For he claims to know things that he doesn't
really know; whereas I neither know nor think that I know. In
this way, I seem to have a slight advantage over him.'

Then I went to another man who had even higher
philosophical pretensions and my conclusion was exactly the
same. I made another enemy of him, and of many others
besides him, as I went from one to another searching for a wise
man.

The truth I learned, O people of Athens, is this: only God
is wise. God's revelation to me was meant to be humbling. He
was using me as an illustration, as if to say: 'the wisest person is
the one who, like Socrates, knows that his "wisdom" is in truth
worth nothing.'

As demonstrated in this passage, the elenchus is a powerful
way to refute your opponent. It is therefore useful, not just in
court, but in any philosophical debate.

We can appreciate the structure of the argument more clearly
if we rewrite it in schematic form as follows:

To Prove: Socrates is the wisest person.

1. Suppose Socrates is not the wisest person.

2. If Socrates is not the wisest person, then other people
must be wiser.

3. All the other people claim to know things they don't
really know.

4. It would be absurd for a wise person to claim to know
things he or she doesn't really know.

---

5. Therefore, Socrates is the wisest person.

Notice that if you accept steps (1) through (4), then you can't deny step (5). In the middle ages, this method of argumentation came to be called '*reductio ad absurdum*,' which is Latin for 'reduction to an absurdity.' It is still widely used today. The goal is not to show that your opponent is silly or laughable, but rather to show that his view implies something that cannot possibly be true. In philosophy, the word 'absurdity' refers to an impossibility or contradiction.

Validity

Although Socrates typically preferred to use the elenchus method in his arguments, Plato's student Aristotle realized that there are a number of other equally compelling ways to make one's case. In the following passage from a work called *Prior Analytics*, Aristotle develops a general criterion for classifying and evaluating different kinds of arguments.

LOGIC BASICS

A 'premise' is a statement affirming or denying one thing with respect to another. It must be universal, particular, or indefinite. By 'universal' I mean the statement that something belongs to all or none of something else; by 'particular' I mean the statement that something belongs to some, or not to some, or not to all of something else.

A 'syllogism' is an argument in which, certain things being stated (the premises), something other than what is stated (the conclusion) follows of necessity from their being so. That is, the premises produce the conclusion: no further term is required from without in order to make the conclusion necessary.

First, take a 'universal negative' premise using the terms A and B. If no B is A, neither can any A be B. For if some A (say C) were B, it would not be true that no B is A; for C is a B.

Next, consider a "universal positive." If every B is A, then some A is B. If no A were B, then no B could be A. But we assumed that every B is A.

Now take a 'particular positive' syllogism with the terms A and B. If some B is A, then some of the As must be B. If none were, then no B would be A.

Finally, if some B is not A, then there is no necessity that some of the As should not be B; e.g. let B stand for animal and A for human being. Not every animal is a human being; but every human being is an animal. This is a 'particular negative' syllogism.

In this groundbreaking exposition Aristotle defines the crucial concept of 'syllogism,' which medieval philosophers later called '**deductive validity**,' from the Latin verbs *deducere,* meaning 'to lead down,' and *valere,* meaning 'to be strong or successful.' The conclusion of a deductively valid argument *follows from* its premises with necessity.

The necessity of a deductively valid inference is evident in the four types of arguments Aristotle discusses. We should examine them in closer detail.

1. Universal Negative

No apple (A) is a banana (B).

This sentence says that the set of apples does not intersect with the set of bananas.

As the diagram shows, the sentence clearly supports the further inference Aristotle draws, that if no A is B, then no B is A.

2. Universal Positive

Every bug (B) is an annoyance (A).

This sentence says that the set of bugs is a subset of the set of annoyances.

As the diagram shows, the sentence clearly supports the further inference Aristotle draws, that if every B is an A, then some A is a B.

3. Particular Positive

Some boy (B) is an African (A).

This sentence says that at least one boy is a member of the set of Africans.

We don't know from the sentence whether B intersects with A or is a subset of A. These two possibilities are represented with dotted circles on the diagram. All we know for sure, as Aristotle infers, is that if some B is A, then some A must be B.

4. Particular Negative

Some animal (B) is not a human being (A).

This sentence says that the set of animals is not a subset of the set of human beings.

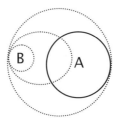

As Aristotle notes, the sentence *does not* support the inference that some of the As are not Bs. As the dotted circles on the diagram show, we can't tell from the sentence whether A is a subset of B, or whether it intersects, or whether it does not intersect at all.

This failure of inference makes a crucial point. When Aristotle defines 'syllogism' in the above passage he says that the premises must produce the conclusion in such a way that 'no further term is required from without in order to make the conclusion necessary.' Obviously, we all know that the set of human beings is a subset of the set of animals. But logic does not allow us to import information from the outside to arrive at a conclusion. This would be like saying 2 + 2 = 5 because we can always add a 1 from somewhere else!

Aristotle discusses many more different types of syllogism. In so doing he established that there is a mathematical certainty to logic just like any equation in arithmetic. In a deductively valid argument the premises must imply their conclusion in such a way that, if the premises are true, then the conclusion has to be true. This is to say that the premises 'add up' to their conclusion in the same way that 2 + 2 = 4.

Aristotle in turn had two students named Theophrastus (*c.* 371–*c.* 278 BC) and Eudemus (dates unknown) who worked together to improve and expand on the growing body of logic. Their most important contribution was to introduce the notion of a 'conditional' statement within an argument. A **conditional statement** is an 'if-then' statement. For example:

If it is raining, then the streets are wet.

Notice that a conditional statement has two parts. The 'if' part is called the 'antecedent' and the 'then' part is called the 'consequent.'

People use conditional statements all the time to make their case. In fact, when you look at ordinary, everyday reasoning, an identifiable pattern in three steps emerges again and again. The first step is a premise in the form of a conditional statement; the second step is a premise affirming the antecedent of the conditional; the third step is a conclusion inferring the consequent of the conditional. Theophrastus and Eudemus schematized this pattern as follows:

1. If something is P, then it is Q.
2. x is P.

---

3. Therefore, x is Q.

We can generate an example using this pattern as follows:

1. If someone is a logician, then he is a philosopher.
2. Theophrastus and Eudemus were logicians.

---

3. Therefore, Theophrastus and Eudemus were philosophers.

Notice that this is a deductively valid inference. Regardless of what sentences you plug into the pattern, the truth of the premises will imply the truth of the conclusion. In the middle ages, this argument form came to be called '***modus ponens***,' which is Latin shorthand for 'the method of affirming the antecedent of the conditional.'

Another very common pattern of reasoning is closely related to modus ponens. The first step is, again, a premise in the form of a conditional statement; the second step, however, is a premise denying the consequent of the conditional; the third step is a conclusion inferring the denial of the antecedent. Theophrastus and Eudemus schematized this pattern as follows:

1. If something is P, then it is Q.
2. x is not Q.

---

3. Therefore, x is not P.

Once again, we can generate an example using this pattern as follows:

1. If someone is a logician, then he is a philosopher.
2. Caesar was not a philosopher.

---

3. Therefore, Caesar was not a logician.

Notice that this too is a deductively valid inference. Regardless of what sentences you plug into the pattern, the truth of the premises will guarantee the truth of the conclusion. Medieval philosophers came to refer to this argument form as '*modus tollens*,' which is Latin shorthand for 'the method of denying the consequent of the conditional.'

Theophrastus proceeded on his own to develop a third argument form using the conditional statement. The pattern is as follows:

1. If something is X, then it is Y.
2. If something is Y, then it is Z.

---

3. Therefore, if something is X, then it is Z.

This argument form, also deductively valid, has come to be known as '**hypothetical syllogism**' because it is 'iffy' all the way down to the conclusion.

Hypothetical syllogism is especially useful because the steps can be iterated as many times as you like. Consider the following argument:

1. If Aristotle was a logician, then he was a philosopher.
2. If he was a philosopher, then he was educated.
3. If he was educated, then he was smart.

4. If he was smart, then he was happy.

---

5. Therefore, if Aristotle was a logician, then he was happy.

As you can see, the conclusion connects the antecedent of premise (1) to the consequent of premise (4) by what we call the law of transitivity.

Furthermore, modus ponens can be combined with hypothetical syllogism to produce a more definite conclusion, as in the following example:

1. If Aristotle was a logician, then he was a philosopher.
2. If he was a philosopher, then he was educated.
3. If he was educated, then he was smart.
4. If he was smart, then he was happy.
5. Aristotle was a logician.

(Affirms the antecedent of step 1)

---

6. Therefore, Aristotle was happy.

(Infers the consequent of step 4)

In general, any deductively valid argument forms can be combined as long as their rules of inference are strictly followed. This is how philosophers make their case on complex issues.

Here is one more useful argument form from both Theophrastus and Eudemus:

1. Something is either F or G.
2. It is not F.

---

3. Therefore, it is G.

Today we know this style of reasoning as 'process of elim-ination.' We can create a familiar example as follows:

1. The killer is either a doctor or a lawyer.
2. The killer is not a doctor.

---

3. Therefore, the killer is a lawyer.

This argument form has come to be called '**disjunctive syllogism**' because the 'either-or' in the first line is a disjunct of possibilities. Notice that the disjunct can include as many possibilities as you want as long as you eliminate them accordingly.

Soundness and fallacies

By now it should be evident that validity concerns the structure of the argument only while ignoring the content. It means that *if* all the premises are true, then the conclusion has to be true; it does not guarantee that the premises are in fact true. This did not go unnoticed by ancient philosophers.

Chrysippus (*c.* 280–207 BC) was a student at the Stoic school. Concerned to call attention to the fact that good logic does not necessarily result in a good theory, Chrysippus established the crucial distinction between validity and soundness.

STOICISM

Stoicism is the school of thought founded by Zeno of Citium just before 300 BC. It spread from the Greek golden age into the Roman Empire and lasted hundreds of years. The Stoics get their name from the Greek word for 'porch' because in the early days they met on a porch in the public square in Athens.

The Stoics believed that all emotion arises from false judgment. They therefore strove always to avoid fear, anger, love, or passion of any kind. This practice is reflected in our modern adjective, 'stoical.'

According to Stoicism, reason is the only path to true freedom. Stoics therefore studied logic and contributed important insights to logical theory.

For example, consider the following argument:

1. All philosophers are happy.
2. Socrates was a philosopher.

─────────────────────────────

3. Therefore, Socrates was happy.

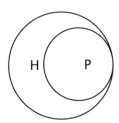

There is no denying that this argument is valid. The first premise is a universal positive that can be represented in the following diagram, where H stands for happy people and P stands for philosophers.

The second premise adds another circle, marked S, for Socrates.

Notice that, without adding anything else, the conclusion is already present in the diagram. This is how we know it is valid. The conclusion is implicit in the premises. Once the premises are laid out, there is no avoiding the conclusion: Socrates was happy. This is to say that if the premises are true, then the conclusion has to be true.

Although the structure of the argument is flawless, you might disagree with the content. For example, you might object to premise (1) which states that all philosophers are happy. Perhaps you can think of a philosopher who isn't happy at all. This would be a counterexample to premise (1). Counterexamples give you a basis for rejecting the argument even while recognizing that its logic is good. In this case, you would say that the argument is valid but unsound. **Soundness** is the highest praise for an argument. If you judge an argument to be sound, this means you think it is valid and all of its premises are true.

When Chrysippus originally proposed this distinction he said that an argument can be valid but 'untrue.' Using the term 'untrue' proved to be confusing though because you might reject an argument even though you think some of its steps are true. For example, in the above argument, premise (2) is true: Socrates was a philosopher. So to call the argument as a whole 'untrue' is misleading. Later philosophers came to use the term 'unsound' instead in order to make it clear that you only need to disagree with one premise in order to reject it.

After Chrysippus we have no record of further development in logic until we come to the Turkish physician and philosopher, Galen (AD 129–*c.* 216). Galen's main interest lay in the practice of medicine. He was disturbed by the extent to which other physicians he knew of used poor reasoning in treating illness. He wrote a book that attempted to identify and explain common logical mistakes. The book is called *Fallacies* in English, because a **fallacy** is a mistake in reasoning.

According to Galen, the fundamental error of medicine occurs due to confusion between labelling and diagnosis. Suppose a patient arrives with three symptoms: fever, rash, and nausea. The doctor consults his sources and determines that these are symptoms of Disease X. Now the doctor has a handy label to focus on. Rather than treating the patient, he treats Disease X. Galen contends that any doctor who uses a label in this way misses his target and will only succeed by accident if he succeeds at all. For Galen, true diagnosis requires focusing on the patient himself as a unique individual.

The confusion between labelling and diagnosis is a common error in philosophy as well. Today known as the '**fallacy of the straw man**,' it occurs when an author refutes a simplistic substitute for his opponent's argument rather than the argument itself. A straw man is a scarecrow. It's easy to knock a scarecrow down and doing so is not very impressive. If you want to make an impression you have to target a real person instead.

The straw man fallacy is just one of many mistakes in reasoning that medieval philosophers learned to guard against. We will run into a few on our medieval tour.

Before embarking we need to take a closer look at the diverging philosophies of Plato and Aristotle as an underlying basis for the disagreement among our authors.

Plato's innatism

Almost none of the works of Plato were available in medieval Europe until the end of the middle ages. Despite this, most of Plato's ideas were transmitted to Europe through secondary sources, such as the Roman orator Cicero, and in fact came to dominate early medieval philosophy.

The one work of Plato that was available in medieval Europe, at least in part, was the *Timaeus*. Named for its main character, it is a dialogue concerning cosmology. Cosmology is the systematic study of the origin and nature of the universe. The *Timaeus* represents one of the first surviving attempts to understand the universe scientifically. Although it covers a broad range of topics, our interest lies in the extent to which it demonstrates Plato's innatist epistemology.

PLATO c. 427–347 BC

Plato was born into a rich and powerful family in Athens. Talented as a writer from a young age, he planned to become a playwright until he met the notorious troublemaker Socrates and became his most devoted fan.

Plato wrote a record of Socrates's trial and execution in dialogue form and went on to reconstruct many of Socrates's other debates and conversations. These dialogues are classics of world literature because they are beautifully written and contain momentous ideas that influenced the history of Western civilization.

Resolving to devote himself to the cause for which Socrates sacrificed his life, Plato established a school where adults could continue to explore the philosophical questions Socrates raised. He called it the 'Academy.' Ever since then, the word 'academic' has come to be associated with higher learning.

Epistemology is the branch of philosophy that studies the nature of knowledge. Needless to say, knowledge is a very valuable thing. Everyone claims to have some knowledge at least some of the time. Sometimes you really have knowledge, while other times you only *think* you have knowledge. For example, Jane yelled at Pete because she thought she knew he ate the last cookie, when in fact it was somebody else. Philosophers point out that it would be really useful to have a reliable way of telling the difference between knowing something and only thinking you know it. In order to tell the difference we need to figure out where knowledge comes from.

There are two opposing theories: **innatism** holds that knowledge comes from reasoning within the mind, while **empiricism** holds that knowledge comes from observation of the world. Innatists would say that Jane made a mistake in reasoning, while empiricists would say she was insufficiently observant. We will look at empiricism in detail in connection with Aristotle. Let's turn now to Plato's innatism.

Plato argues repeatedly and with fervour that knowledge comes from reasoning within the mind. He considers mathematics to be the ultimate paradigm for all knowledge. In a dialogue called the *Meno*, he contends that knowledge has to come from reasoning within our own minds or else we couldn't explain how people are able to figure out the solutions to math problems all by themselves. How do you know that 2 + 2 = 4? Do you need to count apples? No. You simply think about it and see that it cannot be wrong. In Plato's view, this is the way it is for all knowledge, even though, once you go beyond arithmetic, it becomes difficult to see. We human beings are born with the truth stamped upon our souls, but we spend our lives trying to figure out how to access it.

Plato applies his innatist epistemology in the *Timaeus*. In the passage we will be examining he is attempting to answer two questions:

1. Is the world round?
2. Does the world move?

These questions may strike you as funny because today we have answered them beyond a shadow of a doubt. Yet, in the ancient world, these questions were controversial. It is commonly asserted that everyone believed the world was flat before Christopher Columbus 'discovered' America. While it may be the case that many uneducated people thought this, many philosophers were convinced otherwise.

In the passage below from the *Timaeus*, Plato makes arguments for his answers to the above questions.

THE BEST MAKES THE BEST

Let me tell you why God made this world. God is good, and the good can never be jealous of anything. Being free from jealousy, God desired that all things should be as much like himself as they could be. God is the best and the deeds of the best could never be or have been other than the fairest.

When God looked around he found a mass of chaos moving in an irregular and disorderly fashion. Out of the disorder he brought order, considering that order was in every way better than disorder.

God judged that the shape most suitable for the world would be that which comprehends within itself all other shapes. So he made the world in the form of a sphere, round as from a lathe. The sphere has its extremes in every direction equidistant from the centre. This is the most perfect and the most like itself of all figures. God chose it because he considered that the like is infinitely fairer than the unlike.

Then God assigned the movement suited to this spherical form. Of all the seven types of movement, he chose that which is most appropriate to mind and intelligence. So he made the world move in the same manner and on the same spot, within its own limits, rotating in a circle. He deprived it of all of the other six types of motion.

Although everything was once without reason and measure, God fashioned everything by form and number. Let us consistently maintain in all we say that God made the world as far as possible the fairest and best out of things that were not fair. Everywhere God has exactly perfected the ratios of their numbers, motions, and other properties, and harmonized them in due proportion.

Plato's answer to our first question is evident in the third paragraph when he says God 'made the world in the form of a sphere, round as from a lathe.' So, as it turns out, Plato got the answer right. The interesting question for us, however, is: How did he arrive at this answer? Recall that Plato had no photographs from outer space, no ocean-worthy ship, not even a telescope to help him. Plato didn't use observation to come to his conclusion at all. His argument is innatist because it is built on pure reason.

The fundamental reason Plato employs to arrive at the correct conclusion is the notion of divine perfection. The notion of divine perfection is innatist rather than empiricist because it is an abstraction; i.e. it is not observable in the world. It may seem strange at first to use the notion of divine perfection to draw scientific conclusions. But notice how Plato explicitly connects the notion of divine perfection to measure, number, and proportion. Plato is advancing the thesis that there is a fundamentally mathematical order to reality that is accessible to the mind alone. Later innatists would describe this order in terms of the physical laws of the universe.

One way to reconstruct Plato's first argument is to use transitive reasoning as follows:

1. The world is perfect in every way.
2. The perfect shape is the sphere.

---

3. Therefore, the world is a sphere.

Notice, however, that forcing Plato's reasoning into just three steps oversimplifies it. We could extend the argument in a more comprehensive way as follows:

1. If God made the world, then it is perfect in every way.
2. God made the world.
3. So, the world is perfect in every way.
4. The perfect shape is the one most like itself.
5. The shape most like itself is the one whose sides are equidistant.
6. The shape whose sides are equidistant is the sphere.

---

7. Therefore, the world is a sphere.

This argument is deductively valid by a combination of modus ponens and transitivity. Although the logic is good and the conclusion is correct, the premises are highly controversial.

Someone who did not agree with Plato's assumption that divine perfection underlies the structure of the cosmos might reject the soundness of the argument even if she agrees with the conclusion.

What about the second question: Does the world move? Plato answers this question in the fourth paragraph above when he writes that God 'made the world move in the same manner and on the same spot, within his own limits, rotating in a circle.' Right again, Plato! Notice, however, that God deprived the world of all other motions. So, in Plato's view, the earth rotates (spins on its axis) but it does not revolve (move around the sun). To this extent Plato was wrong. Nevertheless, we are interested not so much in his conclusion, but rather, in how he arrives at it.

The second argument is less clear than the first. Still, it is evident that Plato relies heavily on the notion of suitability, harkening back to the notion of perfection that pervades the whole passage and that we featured in our first reconstruction. 'Suitability,' 'proportion,' 'best,' and 'fairest' are all derivatives of perfection that our minds impose on the world through reasoning. This, once again, confirms that Plato's approach is innatist.

We might reconstruct this argument very much like the first as follows:

1. If God made the world, then it is perfect in every way.
2. God made the world.
3. So, the world is perfect in every way.
4. The perfect motion is the one most like itself.
5. The motion most like itself is the one that moves in the same manner, on the same spot, within its own limits.
6. The motion that moves in the same manner, on the same spot, within its own limits is rotation.

---

7. Therefore, the world rotates.

Notice that we took some interpretive licence with this argument in order to make it deductively valid. Leaving out the idea that rotation is the 'motion of intelligence,' we instead supplied the notion of likeness from the paragraph above. This makes the argument fit together in a way that may seem sound to an innatist. Still, it is possible to imagine how someone who did not share Plato's approach might reject it.

We have seen how innatism led Plato to remarkable success on two difficult cosmological questions. His epistemology seems to have produced knowledge. But before you conclude he was right to assert that truth comes from within, let's give Aristotle's empiricism a chance.

Aristotle's empiricism

The only work of Aristotle that was available in Latin translation in medieval Europe before the twelfth century was his work on logic. In the twelfth century, medieval philosophers rediscovered Aristotle's other works and made Latin translations.

ARISTOTLE 384–322 BC

Aristotle was the star student at Plato's Academy. However, Plato's relatives apparently didn't understand that philosophers are *supposed* to disagree. When Plato died, they chose his likeminded nephew to take over the school even though Aristotle was by far the better philosopher.

Consequently, Aristotle left Athens to become the tutor of Alexander the Great. It is said that Alexander was so fond of his teacher that when he went off to war he sent samples of foreign plants and animals back to Aristotle for study.

With Alexander's encouragement, Aristotle established his own school in Athens called the Lyceum. It was nicknamed the 'peripatetic' school, from the Greek words for 'walking around,' because Aristotle liked stroll the gardens with his students while they philosophized.

Aristotle is an empiricist, maintaining that knowledge comes from observation of the world. While Plato was convinced human beings must have all truths stamped upon their souls at birth, Aristotle believes that each human being is born a *tabula rasa* or blank slate. He asserts that information enters our minds through the five senses. If we observe the world carefully, we can learn the truth about it. This is knowledge in his view.

Plato rejected empiricism because he regarded the senses as untrustworthy. How many times have your eyes or your ears deceived you? If they could lead you astray once or twice, then they could lead you astray all the time. Furthermore, our senses tell us about the way things *appear* as opposed to the way things really *are*. Have you ever heard someone say something like this: 'Sally *looks* happy but she really isn't.' How do we make such judgments if knowledge comes from observation? Our eyes tell us one thing, and yet we know it isn't true. For Plato, there is a deeper layer to everything. Only reasoning within the mind will reveal the truth behind the appearance of things.

Aristotle, however, was not so sceptical of the five senses. In his view, it is dangerous to rely on the reasoning within the mind because it is too easy simply to start making things up. How do you know Sally isn't really happy? If this is true, then you must have observed some small sign that tipped you off. If there were no observable signs, then you would have no basis for making such a claim. You could be projecting your own feelings or biases on to her. Avoiding this danger, empiricism forces you to limit yourself to the evidence.

Aristotle applies his empiricist epistemology in his treatise, *On the Heavens*. In the section we will examine he is attempting to answer the same two questions we looked at in Plato's *Timaeus*:

1. Is the world round?
2. Does the world move?

We will see that, although Aristotle only partially disagreed with Plato's conclusions, he completely disagreed with his methodology.

In the passage below, Aristotle makes arguments for his answers to each of the above questions.

OBSERVATIONS OF MOTION AND SHAPE

Let's turn to the questions concerning the motion and shape of the world. There is no general agreement here. Some say it revolves around the centre. Others, including Plato, say it rotates at the centre.

In my view, it is apparent that the world is immobile. Observation shows that it is the nature of earth to move from any point to the centre, just as it is the nature of fire to move in the opposite direction – from the centre to the extremity. It is impossible for any portion of earth to move away from the centre except by force. For, a single thing has a single movement, and a simple thing a simple movement. Contrary movements cannot belong to the same thing, and movement away from the centre is the contrary of movement toward the centre. If then no portion of earth can move away from the centre, obviously still less can the earth as a whole so move. For it is the nature of the whole to move to the point to which the part naturally moves. The world would require a force greater than itself to move it. Therefore, it must necessarily stay at the centre.

The evidence of the senses further corroborates the spherical shape of the world. How else would eclipses of the moon show segments shaped as we see them? As it is, the shapes which the moon itself each month shows are of every kind – straight, convex, and concave – but in eclipses the outline is always curved. Since it is the interposition of the earth that makes the eclipse, the form of this line will be caused by the form of the earth's surface, which is therefore spherical.

Moreover, our observations of the stars make it evident, not only that the world is spherical, but also that it is a sphere of no great size. A small change of position to the south or north causes a manifest alteration of the horizon; i.e. one sees different stars as one moves. Indeed there are some stars seen in Egypt and Cyprus that are not seen in the northerly regions at all.

Aristotle's answer to the first question is evident from the end of the second paragraph, where he says, 'The world would require a force greater than itself to move it. Therefore, it must necessarily stay at the centre.' Ooops – wrong answer, Aristotle. While not directly addressing the question of rotation in this passage, Aristotle is clearly agreeing with Plato's incorrect view that the earth does not revolve.

But notice Aristotle's explicit appeal to observation. His argument hinges on the fact that parts of the earth always fall toward the centre of the earth and cannot move in any other direction by themselves. This is an empiricist talking. We can reconstruct Aristotle's argument in valid form as follows:

1. The whole of any thing can move only the same way as its parts.

2. The parts of the earth move toward the centre.

3. So, the whole of the earth can move only toward the centre.

4. If the whole of the earth can move only toward the centre, then there would need to be a force greater than itself to move it away from the centre.

5. If there would need to be a force greater than the earth itself to move it away from the centre, then the earth cannot move at all.

---

6. Therefore, the earth cannot move at all.

Although Aristotle makes a few other points that may be relevant in defending his premises, these six steps are enough to represent his view. Where does Aristotle go wrong? Premises (1) through (4) are hard to doubt.

Our modern understanding of the solar system, however, puts us in a good position to challenge premise (5). It presupposes that there can be no force greater than the earth itself. But when it comes to the force of gravity, this is incorrect. The amount of gravitational pull of an object is determined by its mass. The sun is more massive than the earth. Therefore, the sun has more gravitational pull than the earth. In fact, we know today that the force of the sun's gravitational pull is precisely what keeps the earth revolving. Aristotle was not able to make the necessary observations for a correct answer to the first question.

Aristotle makes two separate arguments concerning the second question. Let's look at the one at the end of the third paragraph where he says, 'Since it is the interposition of the earth that makes the eclipse, the form of this line will be caused by the form of the earth's surface, which is therefore spherical.' Points for Aristotle on this one! Notice once again Aristotle's empiricist appeal to the evidence of the senses.

We can represent this argument as follows:

1. If the earth were not spherical, then it would not project a curved shadow on the moon during an eclipse.

2. But the earth does project a curved shadow on the moon during an eclipse.

---

3. Therefore, the earth is spherical.

This argument is valid by modus tollens. Although it is short, it captures Aristotle's reasoning effectively.

Even though modern science confirms the soundness of this argument, it is useful to see how someone might object to it. There is still today a group of people known as the 'Flat Earth Society' who deny that the earth is a sphere. (You can find them on the Internet.) Which premise of this argument might they object to, and how would Aristotle respond?

We have seen that Aristotle was more interested in the nitty-gritty details of science than was Plato, who preferred to explore ideal patterns. While Aristotle is most famous for inventing the system of genus and species that is still used around the world to categorize plants and animals, Plato is most famous for imagining a system of justice that has inspired great leaders through the ages. So, in some ways it was appropriate for Aristotle to be an empiricist while Plato was an innatist.

You may be thinking at this moment: Surely you need both – empiricism for concrete studies and innatism for abstract concepts.

Before you walk away satisfied with this pronouncement, be warned: combining opposite theories is not as easy as you might think. The worst error in philosophy is to adopt two ideas that contradict each other, because self-contradictory theories have no chance of being true. The hybrid theory, which we might call 'innato-empiricism,' can avoid self-contradiction only by carefully establishing a criterion for determining which knowledge comes from reasoning within the mind and which knowledge comes from observation of the world. Establishing this criterion is a difficult chore!

Having said this, it is perhaps more useful to think of innatism and empiricism as lying at two ends of a single continuum.

Innatism   Empiricism

Some philosophers will be extremists on either side, while others will fall somewhere in between the two. It is interesting to see where each philosopher falls and why. We have seen that Plato lands on the innatist side while Aristotle lands on the empiricist side. We will see the rest of the authors in this book take their place on the continuum as we embark on our tour of the middle ages.

2
Ontological proof of God

> I do not try to understand in order to believe;
> I believe in order to understand.
>
> Anselm

In the second century AD, the Egyptian philosopher Plotinus founded the school of thought known as **neoplatonism**, which developed a mystical interpretation of Plato. A strong theme among neoplatonic thinkers is disdain for the material world. In Plato's view, the material world is full of illusion and is inferior to the intelligible world of truths that are accessible only through reasoning within the mind.

Plotinus was one of the most significant influences on Augustine, a figure of towering importance throughout the middle ages. Augustine is considered the founder of Christian neoplatonism, which provided fertile ground for his successor Anselm as well.

Throughout the early middle ages, philosophers just weren't very interested in a posteriori truths, meaning truths that come from experience of the material world. Augustine and Anselm maintain that the most important truth, namely, the truth about God, is a priori, meaning 'prior to experience.' They both present proofs of the existence of God that depend on reason alone, without any reference to the external world. They are excellent studies in innatism.

The doctrine of illumination

The notion that the material world is not to be trusted appealed to Augustine's Christian sympathies. According to his interpretation of the Bible, the present life is really nothing but a brief ordeal that we must endure on our way to the next life, hopefully in heaven.

Augustine wrote a monumental book called *City of God* in which he argues that there are two kinds of people: (1) members of the City of God set their sights on heaven and avoid being distracted by the material world; (2) members of the City of Man,

AUGUSTINE AD 354–430

Augustine had the bad luck of having to live his life through the end of the Roman Empire.

He was born in a small town on the Mediterranean coast in North Africa, which was part of the Roman Empire at this time. His father worked for the Roman government. During Augustine's childhood, the Roman Empire seemed strong and life was good.

Augustine showed promise as a student and was given a quality education in Latin, though he never did learn Greek. His father was a pagan after the traditional Roman fashion, but his mother was a Christian. Through his youth, Augustine enjoyed a raucous lifestyle. He hung out with troublemakers, he liked to party, and he even fathered an illegitimate child. Around the age of thirty, however, he had a religious experience that convinced him to become a Christian.

As Augustine grew older, life on the Mediterranean coast deteriorated. The Roman Empire weakened and soon barbarian warriors invaded. The people of Hippo, a city near his birthplace, begged Augustine to be their Bishop. Though reluctant, he agreed, and offered them spiritual comfort and leadership as the Roman Empire fell to pieces around them. He was eventually canonized as a saint by the Catholic Church.

in contrast, get caught up in the material world and lose sight of heaven. Augustine cautions that you will never be able to tell exactly which people are members of which city because membership is determined by the internal state of the person, which only God can judge. Needless to say, Augustine recommends striving as hard as you possibly can to be a member of the City of God. You cannot be both worldly and godly. You have to choose.

Given this dramatic picture of the situation, it is not surprising that Augustine took Plato's innatism very seriously. For Augustine, it is not just an epistemology but the only avenue to salvation. Finding the truth within you is the only way to find God. Rather than simply taking this idea for granted as an assumption, however, Augustine makes a very interesting argument for it. You will find it in the passage below from a work called *On the Teacher*.

THE TEACHER WITHIN

Sometimes we perceive things through the mind, that is, through intellect and reason. When we 'see' things in the inner light of truth, we illuminate the inner person. If someone who is listening to us 'sees' what we are talking about with his inner 'eye,' then he knows what we are saying from his own contemplation, not from our words.

Sometimes someone will deny something when questioned about it but then later admit it after further questions. This happens because of the weakness of his discernment. His inner light is not bright enough to shine over the whole matter. Yet further questions enable him to illuminate it part-by-part. The words of the questioner guide him but do not teach him. They raise questions in such a way that he learns from within, in accordance with his ability.

For example, suppose I were to ask you about the very matter at hand, namely, where does knowledge come from? At first the topic would seem absurd to you, since you aren't able to examine it as a whole. It would therefore be necessary for me to ask you questions that would enable you to hear the Teacher within you. Thus I might say: 'Consider the things you claim to know – where did you learn them?' Maybe you would reply that I taught them to you. Then I would respond: 'What if I say I saw a flying man? Could I just as easily make you learn that there are flying men?' Surely you would deny it and reply that you do not believe that I saw a flying man. Even if you were willing to say you believed me, you wouldn't say you knew it to be true. As a result, you would then understand that you hadn't learned anything from my words.

Likewise, it doesn't help to teach those who cannot see with the inner eye. They will hear what you're saying and perhaps even believe you without ever achieving knowledge of their own. Yet those who do see with the inner eye are students of the truth within. They are in a position to judge what the speaker says. Often they know the truth about what is said even when the speaker doesn't. For example, suppose someone who doesn't believe in the soul is reciting arguments for the existence of the soul. The speaker is unaware that he's stating truths – he thinks he's stating falsehoods. Should it then be thought that he teaches what he doesn't know? Yet he uses the very same words that someone who does know also could use.

Augustine's innatism is known as the 'doctrine of illumination' because he speaks of knowledge as an inner light.

Augustine loves to use rhetorical questions to provoke his reader. We see two in the above passage and we know that important points are being made in each case. Let's look at the following section of the passage: 'Thus I might say: "Consider the things you claim to know – where did you learn them?" Maybe you would reply that I taught them to you. Then I would respond: "What if I say I saw a flying man? Could I just as easily make you learn that there are flying men?"' With this last question, Augustine is setting himself up for an argument in the form of modus tollens. We can represent it as follows.

1. If knowledge comes from teachers, then a teacher could make students learn that there are flying men.

2. But a teacher can't make students learn that there are flying men.

---

3. Therefore, knowledge does not come from teachers.

Although this argument is valid, it only delivers us a negative conclusion. We wanted a positive answer to the question, where does knowledge come from? We can get one by adding a disjunctive syllogism step as follows:

1. If knowledge comes from teachers, then a teacher could make students learn that there are flying men.

2. But a teacher can't make students learn that there are flying men.

3. So, knowledge does not come from teachers.

4. Either knowledge comes from teachers, or it comes from within.

---

5. Therefore, knowledge comes from within.

This argument delivers the innatist conclusion Augustine endorses. Moreover, the argument is valid. But is it sound?

Premises (1) and (2) seem fairly solid, making it difficult to deny the subconclusion, (3). Premise (4), however, is weak. Do two options exhaust the possibilities here?

Whenever someone presents you with a choice between two options, you should always ask yourself whether there might be a third that has not been mentioned. This rule underlies the mistake in reasoning known as the **fallacy of false dilemma**, where multiple alternatives are arbitrarily reduced to two. Based on what we saw in the last chapter we can be sure Aristotle would have a third suggestion. In Aristotle's view, knowledge comes neither from teachers nor from within but from the experience of the five senses.

Augustine's proof of the existence of God

In reading the above passage, you may have noticed that Augustine refers to the truth within us as the 'inner Teacher.' This is because he thinks that the ultimate source of all human knowledge is God. God implants truths in human souls and illuminates it for those who search their souls faithfully. Augustine's philosophy – not just here but in almost every facet – depends heavily on the existence of God. It seems reasonable, therefore, to demand proof that God exists. Augustine did his best to deliver on this demand.

The passage below comes from a work called *On Free Choice of the Will,* which Augustine frames as a dialogue between himself and his friend Evodius. Like the passage we just examined, it focuses on the nature of truth.

GOD AND TRUTH

We have been discussing truth at great length. Although it is singular, we have discerned so many things from it. Do you think then that truth is superior to, equal to, or inferior to our minds?

Suppose truth were inferior to our minds. Then we would not judge according to it. Rather, we would subject it to our judgment. We subject physical things to our judgment because they are inferior to us. For example, we commonly say, 'this is not as white or as square as it should be,' or some such. And we judge these matters according to inner rules of truth that we have in common. But we don't judge the rules themselves. For example, when someone says that eternal things are better than temporal things or that seven plus three equals ten, no one says that it shouldn't be so. So, truth is not inferior to our minds.

Suppose truth were equal to our minds. Then, like our minds, it would be changeable. For the mind sees the truth sometimes more and sometimes less. Therefore, it changes. The truth, in contrast, is neither enhanced when we see it more nor is it diminished when we see it less. Furthermore, we can say of a mind that it understands less than it should of the truth. But we can't say of the truth that it is less understandable than it should be. So, truth is not equal to our minds.

Since truth is neither inferior nor equal to our minds it must be superior.

You have agreed, however, that if I could show you something superior to our minds, you would concede that it is God, as long as there is nothing higher still. I have proven that truth is superior to our minds. So you must now grant my conclusion. For, if there is something superior to truth, then that is God, but if not, then the truth itself is God. Either way, you can't deny that God exists, which was the question we set for our discussion.

You may be troubled by this proof given that we have accepted the existence of God by faith. You may think we should hold on to this belief in faith and not seek a logical proof. But relax. God exists, truly and supremely. We can hold this truth by faith and also by knowledge, even if the knowledge is harder to grasp.

Although this passage is not considered one of the greatest proofs of the existence of God, it is important because it inspired one of the greatest, namely, Anselm's, which we will examine later.

We can reconstruct Augustine's argument in valid form as follows:

1. Truth is either inferior to, equal to, or superior to our minds.

2. Truth is not inferior to our minds because then we would judge it.

3. Truth is not equal to our minds because then it would change like our minds.

4. So, truth is superior to our minds.

5. If truth is superior to our minds, then either truth is God or God is superior to truth.

6. If either truth is God or God is superior to truth, then God exists.

---

7. Therefore, God exists.

This argument is valid by disjunctive syllogism and modus ponens. Augustine and his friend Evodius both considered it unquestionably sound even though premise (5) makes a highly questionable assumption that is left unjustified.

Notice how Augustine's proof is purely innatist. He doesn't rely on observation of the world for evidence that God must exist. Rather, he appeals to the idea of hierarchy: God has to exist in order to fill the highest rank in the universe. We don't experience this hierarchy. Rather, it is something reason imposes on the world.

It might seem odd to ask whether truth is superior to, equal to, or inferior to the mind, but such comparisons became a common theme in medieval philosophy. This theme grew into a distinctive picture of the universe that has come to be known as 'the great chain of being.'

The **great chain of being** is a cosmic scale according to which the absolute value of every existing thing can be measured. In its barest outline, it looks something like this:

God
Angels
Human Beings
Animals
Plants
Rocks

On this scale, angels are superior to humans, humans are superior to animals, and so on. There are rankings within each category as well. In fact, anything you can think of has its own rightful place and medieval philosophers often debated the rightful places of things.

We can ultimately trace the great chain of being back to Plato's notion of perfection. Suppose someone asked you to decide whether an apple is better than an orange. Your immediate question should be, 'Better for what?' The comparison is absurd unless you have some criterion by which to judge. For example, if the criterion is 'sources of vitamin C' then the orange will rank higher than the apple, but if the criterion is 'favourite pie ingredient,' then the apple will rank higher than the orange. But these two criteria are of limited application. How do we generate a criterion that provides a single ranking for everything once and for all? The only way is to establish a perfect exemplar. If there is a perfect exemplar, then everything else can be compared to it, and valued accordingly. God, of course, is needed to fill the role of perfect exemplar.

The origin of the notion of the great chain of being reveals a fundamental problem with Augustine's proof. In order to prove the existence of God, Augustine needs to prove that there is a cosmic hierarchy. And in order to prove that there is a cosmic hierarchy, he needs a perfect exemplar against which to compare everything. But the perfect exemplar is God, whose existence he was trying to prove! This is a classic example of circular reasoning – where one of your premises presupposes your conclusion. Medievals called this fallacious form of reasoning *petitio principii* which means 'begging the question.' The **fallacy of begging the question** occurs when you assume the very thing you're trying to prove.

Augustine might respond that he was not so much trying to prove that God exists but only to explain God's place in an orderly conception of the cosmos. Someone who already believed in the great chain of being might, through Augustine's proof, come to see why it implies the existence of God.

Someone who saw the universe as a chaotic accident, in contrast, would not be convinced by his proof. But Augustine would probably not be very interested in trying to convince such a person. As he indicates at the end of the above passage, he thinks of his theological investigations as an exercise in faith seeking understanding. Without some level of faith as a basis, no true intellectual progress can be made in his view.

Anselm's ontological proof

Augustine's closest follower, Anselm, was an eleventh-century Benedictine monk. While Anselm granted the importance of

ANSELM 1033–1109

Anselm was born in Northern Italy. In his mid-twenties he set off traveling and eventually decided to join the Benedictine Order at the monastery of Bec in northern France. Like most monasteries during the middle ages, Bec was a rare center of learning amidst a sea of illiteracy. It soon became evident that Anselm had a great deal of talent as a philosopher. He wrote and taught and, as his reputation grew, he became abbot of the monastery.

In 1093, the king of England invited Anselm to serve as the Archbishop of Canterbury. Anselm reluctantly accepted. Although he became entangled in a number of political controversies, he continued to write philosophical treatises. After his death, he was canonized as a saint by the Catholic Church.

Following Augustine, Anselm made 'faith seeking understanding' his motto. By this he means that philosophy is neither a threat to faith nor a substitute for it. Rather, it provides rational justification for religious belief. Medieval philosophers used this idea in their defense when the Catholic Church accused them, as it often did, of mapping a road to hell with their theories.

faith, he was convinced that pure reason could produce a proof of the existence of God that would be convincing even to an atheist who has no faith at all. Anselm went digging in his own thoughts for an innatist proof and hit the jackpot.

Anselm's proof is the single most famous philosophical contribution that comes to us from the middle ages. When philosophers today have to pick one medieval argument that is above all others worth knowing about, they typically pick Anselm's proof of the existence of God. Some philosophers accept the proof while others reject it. The one thing they all agree about, however, is that it is a truly ingenious argument that everyone should have the chance to consider.

Anselm's proof of the existence of God is known as the **ontological proof**, from the Greek word 'ontos,' which refers to the nature of being. Anselm proposes that the very definition of God's nature proves that he exists.

This is an ambitious proposal. Although we can use definitions to prove many things, existence is not normally one of them. For example, in geometry, we can use the definition of a triangle, 'three-sided plane figure,' to prove that all triangles have three angles that add to 180 degrees. We cannot, however, use the definition of a triangle to prove that triangles exist. Triangles could just be ideas in our minds. To find out whether they exist in the world, you would have to go out and have a look.

As an innatist, Anselm is convinced that nothing we could ever observe out in the world could prove God exists. He models his proof of the existence of God on a mathematical proof that relies on reason alone. The proof is very concise and deceptively simple. You will find it in the following passage from a work he called the *Proslogium*.

THE GREATEST CONCEIVABLE BEING

God is the greatest conceivable being. Or is there no such being? As it says in *Psalms* 14.1, 'The fool has said in his heart, "there is no God" ' It is one thing for an object to be in the understanding, and another to understand that the object exists. When a painter first conceives of what he will afterwards paint, he has it in his understanding, but he does not yet understand it to be, because he has not yet painted it. After he has made the painting, however, he has it in his understanding and he understands that it exists, because he has made it.

Hence, even the 'fool' mentioned in *Psalms* is convinced that something exists in the understanding, namely, the greatest conceivable being. For, when he hears of this, he understands it. And whatever is understood exists in the understanding.

But it seems to me that the greatest conceivable being cannot exist in the understanding alone. For, suppose it exists in the understanding alone. Then it would still be possible for it to exist both in the understanding and in reality. And existing in both the understanding and in reality is better than existing in the understanding alone. So the greatest conceivable being that exists in the understanding alone is not the greatest conceivable being after all.

Therefore, if the greatest conceivable being exists in the understanding alone, then it is not the greatest conceivable being. But obviously this is impossible. Hence, the greatest conceivable being must exist both in the understanding and in reality.

The greatest conceivable being cannot be conceived not to exist!

For, no one who understands what fire and water are can conceive fire to be water. Although someone could say the words 'fire is water,' he could never actually understand them to be true. Likewise, no one who understands what God is can conceive that God does not exist, even if he says these words in his heart.

As is evident from this passage, Anselm wishes to prove the existence of God to an atheist who says in his heart that there is no God.

Anselm's proof stems from his definition of God as 'the greatest conceivable being.' By this he means that God has all of the characteristics that make a being great. We can call these **'great-making characteristics**.' For example, according to the traditional conception, God is omniscient (all-knowing), omnibenevolent (all-loving), and omnipotent (all-powerful). If God were lacking in knowledge, love, or power, he wouldn't be the supreme being of the universe. But these are just three of God's characteristics; the full list is too long to enumerate. By defining God as the greatest conceivable being, Anselm means to encompass all of the characteristics a being would have to have to be God.

Anselm's first step is to point out that even his opponent, the atheist, will be happy to agree to his definition of God. Atheists understand that if God existed, he would be omniscient, omnipotent, etc. That is, they grant that in order for a being to be God, it would have to have all of the great-making characteristics.

This is all Anselm needs to get his proof rolling. It springs from the thesis that existence in reality is one of the great-making characteristics. We can reconstruct it in *reductio ad absurdum* form as follows:

To Prove: The greatest conceivable being exists in both the understanding and in reality.

1. Suppose the greatest conceivable being exists only in the understanding and not in reality.

2. Existence in reality is one of the great-making characteristics.

3. If the greatest conceivable being exists only in the understanding and not in reality, then it lacks one of the great-making characteristics.

4. If the greatest conceivable being lacks one of the great-making characteristics then it is less than the greatest.

5. But it is absurd for the greatest conceivable being to be less than the greatest.

6. Therefore, the greatest conceivable being exists both in the understanding and in reality.

The absurdity Anselm derives from the atheist's position is a contradiction-in-terms: it is logically impossible for the greatest to be less than the greatest.

It takes a while to get the hang of what Anselm means by existing in the understanding versus existing in reality. We can illustrate the difference through a simple example.

The big secret that every child is unhappy to learn at some point while growing up is that Santa Claus does not exist in reality. There is no jolly old man who flies around the world in a sleigh drawn by reindeer on Christmas Eve to deliver gifts through chimneys. Nevertheless, Santa Claus does exist in the understanding. If you ask just about anybody on the street about Santa Claus, they will know exactly what you are talking about, and they will even be able to close their eyes and picture him in their minds. So Santa Claus exists in the understanding but not in reality.

Atheists think God is just like Santa Claus. People pray to heaven in the same way that children write letters to the North Pole. People go to church to worship God in the same way that children go to the mall to tell Santa what he should bring them for Christmas. The whole elaborate tradition surrounding God is just like the whole elaborate tradition surrounding Christmas: it is nothing more than make-believe. God may seem real in the minds of believers, but this is no different than Santa seeming real in the minds of children. This is the atheist position.

Anselm challenges the atheist position by pointing out a difference between God and Santa Claus. The idea of Santa Claus is not defined as the greatest conceivable being. This means that there is no reason to attribute all the great-making characteristics to him. The idea of God, in contrast, is truly an idea of God only if it is defined as the greatest conceivable being.

This means that if you think of him as lacking one of the great-making characteristics, then you just don't understand what God is. Atheists claim to understand what God is. Therefore, they must attribute all of the great-making characteristics to him. But real existence is one of the great-making characteristics. So, even atheists must attribute real existence to God.

Gaunilo's criticism

Not surprisingly, Anselm's proof made a big splash immediately. While some hailed it as pure genius, others saw it as nothing but a clever trick. Gaunilo was one of Anselm's fellow monks. Playing the devil's advocate for the sake of argument, he circulated this response to Anselm:

ON BEHALF OF THE FOOL

The fool might make this reply:

There could be all sorts of things in my understanding whose existence is uncertain or which do not exist at all.

For example, they say that somewhere in the ocean is an island, which, because of the difficulty, or rather the impossibility, of finding it, is called 'Lost Island.' And they say this island has an inestimable wealth of all manner of riches and delicacies in great abundance. Having no owner or inhabitant, it is more excellent than all other countries inhabited by mankind.

Now if someone should tell me that there is such an island, I should easily understand his words. No problem there. But suppose he went on to say, as if by a logical inference: 'You can no longer doubt that this island which is more excellent than all lands really exists somewhere. For, you have no doubt that it exists in your understanding. And it is more excellent to exist, not just in the understanding alone, but both in the understanding and in reality. For this reason Lost Island must really exist somewhere. If it didn't, then any land which really exists somewhere will be more excellent than it, and so the island already understood by you to be the most excellent will not be the most excellent.'

If someone should try to prove to me by such reasoning that Lost Island truly exists, and that its existence should no longer be doubted, I'd say 'You've got to be kidding!' I wouldn't know who was the greater fool: me for allowing such a 'proof' or him for believing it!

Gaunilo is presenting a parody of Anselm's proof. Using the same argument schema, we can substitute 'island' for 'being,' with the following result:

To Prove: The greatest conceivable island exists in both the understanding and in reality.

1. Suppose the greatest conceivable island exists only in the understanding and not in reality.

2. Existence in reality is one of the great-making characteristics.

3. If the greatest conceivable island exists only in the understanding and not in reality, then it lacks one of the great-making characteristics.

4. If the greatest conceivable island lacks one of the great-making characteristics then it is less than the greatest.

5. But it is impossible for the greatest conceivable island to be less than the greatest.

---

6. Therefore, the greatest conceivable island exists both in the understanding and in reality.

It seems evident that, if an island or any old thing can be substituted for God in Anselm's proof, then it can't be right.

Anselm read Gaunilo's parody, however, and denied that an island or any old thing can be substituted for God in his proof.

Step (4) of the parody asserts that it is impossible for the greatest conceivable island to be less than the greatest. Anselm would insist that this is not true. It is true that it is impossible for the greatest conceivable island to be less than the greatest conceivable *island*. This would be a contradiction in terms. But it's not a contradiction to say that the greatest conceivable island is less than the greatest conceivable *being*. In fact, the greatest conceivable island *is* less than the greatest conceivable being. This is to say that the greatest conceivable island is not defined as having all of the great-making characteristics. So there is no reason to suppose it has the great-making characteristic of real existence. God is the only thing that has to have all of the great-making characteristics, and this is why the proof works only for him.

Aquinas's criticism

While some philosophers side with Anselm and others with Gaunilo, still others have criticized the proof in other ways. Perhaps the most pressing concern is that, on closer inspection, the argument seems to beg the question. Recall that this fallacy involves arguing in a circular fashion by assuming exactly what you're trying to prove.

Anselm begins with the apparently innocuous assumption that God is the greatest conceivable being. He claims this assumption is one that both he and his opponent accept because it is just a definition. It tells us what God would have to be like if he existed. But later it becomes evident that by agreeing to this assumption, the atheist has agreed to far more than just a definition. This is due to an ambiguity surrounding the verb 'is' in the definition 'God is the greatest conceivable being.' Someone who asserts 'God is the greatest conceivable being' could mean one of two things:

(1) God is defined as the greatest conceivable being.

or

(2) God exists as the greatest conceivable being.

Anselm claims that he is only asking the atheist to accept the first interpretation of the sentence. However, he needs the second interpretation in order to make his argument work. This can be seen more easily if we reconstruct the argument in valid transitive form as follows:

1. God is the greatest conceivable being.

2. The greatest conceivable being has all the great-making characteristics.

3. Real existence is one of the great-making characteristics.

---

4. Therefore, God has real existence.

If we interpret premise (1) as 'God is defined as the greatest conceivable being,' then we have to change the conclusion to:

(4) Therefore, God is defined as having real existence.

This, of course, doesn't prove anything. So it seems we need to interpret premise (1) as 'God exists as the greatest conceivable being.' But this is equivalent to what we are trying to prove. In other words, the argument is circular. It begins by asking the opponent to accept the very conclusion he rejects.

Thomas Aquinas is a moderate empiricist from the thirteenth century whom we will meet later. He eloquently articulates this objection to Anselm's ontological proof in the following passage.

AGAINST ANSELM

Perhaps the person who hears the name 'God' does not understand it to signify the greatest conceivable being. After all, some people have believed that God has a body. (For example, the ancient Romans believed in Zeus.) But even supposing everyone did understand the name 'God' to signify 'the greatest conceivable being,' still, it doesn't follow from this that they think that what is signified by that name exists in the real world. Rather it follows only that they think it exists in the intellect's apprehension of it. Only if it is taken as an assumption that the greatest conceivable being exists in reality can it be argued that it exists in reality. But this can't be taken as an assumption because it is not granted by those claiming that God does not exist.

While rejecting Anselm's innatist argument, Aquinas proposes his own empiricist proofs of the existence of God, which we will examine in chapters 5 and 6.

It should be noted that we have simplified Anselm's definition of God for ease of presentation. Anselm originally asserted that 'God is that being than which no greater can be conceived.' This is slightly different than asserting that 'God is the greatest conceivable being.' The latter definition implies that the human mind can actually conceive of God while the former does not.

It seems that both Gaunilo and Aquinas were presupposing the latter definition in their criticisms. After all, Gaunilo compares Anselm's God to an island and Aquinas compares him to Zeus – both of which are actually conceivable by the human mind. Anselm might argue that his original definition of God as 'that than which no greater can be conceived' can rescue him from their comparisons. One way or another, debate over the ontological proof is sure to continue for a long time.

3
Evil

He that is kind is free even if he is a slave;
he that is evil is a slave even if he is a king.

Augustine

Augustine wrote a great many books, some of which were read
for hundreds of years after his death more than any other book
except the Bible. Part of the reason for his enduring popularity
is that he writes passionately about topics that were – and still are
– on a lot of people's minds. In the last chapter we saw how his
admirer Anselm embraced and expanded upon his ideas. In this
chapter, we will see how another one of his admirers, Peter John
Olivi, finds reason to disagree with him.

The problem of suffering

Augustine's favourite topic, which he revisits over and over
again throughout his career, is known as the problem of suffering. The **problem of suffering**, also called the **problem of
evil**, raises a deep and difficult question that every human being
has to face at some point in life: Why do bad things happen to
good people?

When we pose this question in the abstract, it doesn't seem
very significant. In order to appreciate the significance of the
question, you have to think back to a time in your life when you
or someone you love was really suffering. Perhaps it was from a
disease, from an accident, from someone's cruelty, or a combination thereof.

For example, consider a case of child abuse that occurred in Burbank, California, as reported in December 2000 by The Associated Press. Investigators found a twelve-year-old girl who lived in a 'slave setting' for at least two years. The girl was so malnourished that she appeared to be seven or eight years old.

'There was not a part of her body that was not bruised, cut or split open,' the investigating officer said. 'When we see people in this condition, they are usually dead.'

Perhaps a case like this would be easier to take if it was the only one of its kind. The depth of the problem really hits home,

CONFESSIONS c. 400 AD

Augustine wrote his first several works in dialogue form. Just like Plato's, Augustine's dialogues were based on conversations with friends. Augustine's most important work, *Confessions*, lends an interesting twist to this convention. It is a monologue, written as Augustine's prayer to God.

In the *Confessions*, Augustine recounts the story of his life while exploring a number of philosophical issues that arise along the way. This was an entirely new way of writing at the time. The *Confessions* is considered the first autobiography in the history of Western civilization.

The most famous section of the *Confessions* concerns a child-hood memory that Augustine deeply regrets. One night he and a bunch of his buddies stole all the pears from a neighbor's pear tree. Although the pears were ripe and delicious, the boys weren't interested in eating or selling them. Instead, they threw them into a pig sty.

As Augustine reflects on the sheer irrationality of this act, he develops his conception of the nature of evil. True evil is done for its own sake. The same idea was chillingly echoed by Johnny Cash when he sang, "I shot a man in Reno – just to watch him die."

however, when you stop to consider the fact that child abuse occurs every single day in every city all around the world.

Thinking about such things is extremely depressing, but it is the only way to understand the problem of suffering. In such situations, all you can do is ask, 'Why?' Why should the girl from Burbank suffer so much? It just doesn't seem fair, especially considering that she is an innocent child. If anyone should suffer, guilty evildoers should, and yet many of them never do suffer like this girl.

Now if this world is all one big accident, and there is no God, then the problem of suffering is easily solved. Bad things happen to good people and bad people alike by random chance. There is no one out there to ensure that the innocent are protected and the guilty are punished.

If, however, there is a God, then the problem of suffering is not so easily solved. God is supposed to be watching out for us and answering our prayers. How can he let the girl from Burbank and other good people like her suffer so much? How hard would it be for him to rescue her? Not hard at all for God! If we can expect parents to take good care of their children, then a fortiori, we can expect God to take care of his creation.

The problem of suffering was especially challenging for Augustine as a neoplatonist. Recall that, in the *Timaeus*, Plato argued that pure reason can be used to uncover truths about the world precisely because the world is ordered in accordance with a divine perfection. But when you look around at all the suffering in the world, it's hard to see any evidence of divine perfection. If the world is not ordered in accordance with divine perfection, then the mind will not be able to discover truths about it through reason alone.

Because Augustine lived during the decline and fall of the Roman Empire he suffered a great deal himself and witnessed severe suffering around him. For example, his beloved son, Adeodatus, died at age sixteen. Augustine wanted to believe in

God, and did believe, but it seemed to him at times that, if God really exists, the world should be a much better place. The sceptic in him insisted that the unfair distribution of pain and happiness may prove that God does not exist.

We can state the sceptic's argument in a valid form combining hypothetical syllogism and modus tollens as follows:

1. If God exists, then he is omniscient, omnibenevolent, and omnipotent.

2. If God is omniscient, then he knows about suffering.

3. If God is omnibenevolent, then he doesn't want people to suffer.

4. If God is omnipotent, then he can prevent suffering.

5. If God knows about suffering, doesn't want people to suffer, and can prevent it, then there should be no suffering.

6. But there is suffering.

---

7. Therefore, God does not exist.

If you disagree with the conclusion, then you have to dispute one of the premises. But it's hard to see which one might be incorrect.

Premise (1) is presupposed by orthodox Christianity. If you deny that God is omniscient, omnibenevolent, or omnipotent, then you no longer believe in God as standardly defined in mainstream monotheist religions. Premises (2) through (4) are true by definition. And premise (6) is an empirical fact. So it seems that the challenger's best bet lies with premise (5).

Augustine's solution

Early in his career, Augustine developed an argument to show that premise (5) is incorrect. In order to disprove a conditional statement, you have to show that the antecedent could be true while the consequent is false. In other words, you have to show that God could know about suffering, not want it to happen, and be able to prevent it, and yet not prevent it. Augustine thought perhaps God allows suffering because he has good reason.

Augustine's first suggestion was that God has to allow suffering in order to preserve human freedom. God could eliminate a lot of suffering by preventing human beings from being cruel to each other. For example, he could make war, rape, and torture disappear. But these are things that human beings freely choose to do. So, in order to prevent them, he would have to eliminate free will. And if he did that, then human beings would be no better than animals or robots. God judges that free will is so valuable that it is worth the price of the cruelty that some people choose. This solution to the problem of suffering has come to be known as the **free will defence** and it is still very widely accepted.

Augustine realized, however, that the free will defence is inadequate by itself. There are two different types of evil that human beings suffer: natural evils and evil actions. The free will defence explains why God allows people to commit evil actions while saying nothing about natural evils, such as diseases, hurricanes, fires, and other unavoidable accidents. Furthermore, go back to the girl from Burbank. Do you really think that the people who abused her for two years were making a free choice or do you think they were mentally ill? Mental illness is often caused by genetic factors beyond our control and millions of people suffer terribly from it – either directly or indirectly. God could eliminate mental illness completely and make a great number of people happy without interfering with free will at all.

Recognizing this, Augustine supplemented his free will defence. He asserts that, while evil acts are the result of free will, natural evils are God's punishment for evil acts. In other words, God uses diseases, hurricanes, fires, and the like to make us pay for our bad choices. And we don't pay as individuals but rather as a group. Because humanity sins, humanity must pay – the payment need not be matched to the individual sinner.

This is the only way to explain cases like the girl from Burbank. There is no way she could have committed enough evil in her short life to warrant her extreme suffering. So she must be paying for the evil of someone else. How can this be fair? Augustine maintains that because human beings are God's children we are all brothers and sisters. Our souls are inextricably linked. We therefore have to share responsibility for each other.

Suppose Augustine is correct to propose that suffering has to exist given that sinners exist. The question remains: why did God create sinners at all? He could have limited himself to creating a world full of angels just like the archangel Michael, who is both free and good. According to the tradition, Michael is so smart and strong that he always does the right thing. Instead of making a world full of creatures like Michael, God created a world full of weak and stupid human beings with mental illnesses and other flaws that lead to sin. Why did he do it?

In the passage below from *On Free Choice of the Will* Augustine argues that God had a good reason for creating sinners.

UNHAPPINESS

Perhaps someone might say: 'It would not have been terribly difficult or troublesome for an omnipotent God to place all his creatures in such an order that none of them would ever be unhappy. For if he is omnipotent, he could not have lacked the power to do so; and if he is good, he would not have begrudged his creatures such happiness.'

I would reply that the order of creation proceeds from the highest to the lowest by just degrees. It is pure spite to say that something in that creation ought to be different, or shouldn't exist at all. It is wrong to want one thing to be like something else that is superior to it. The superior thing already exists in such a way that it would be wrong to add to it, since it is perfect. Therefore, someone who says 'this thing ought to be like that one' either wants to add to the perfect and superior creature, and so he is immoderate and unjust; or else he wants to destroy the lower creature, and so he is wicked and spiteful.

But someone who says 'this thing ought not to exist' is no less wicked and spiteful, since the thing that he wants not to exist, although inferior, clearly deserves praise. For example, someone might say: 'the moon ought not to exist because it is not as bright as the sun.' Meanwhile, he has to admit that even the light of a lamp, which is not nearly as bright as the sun, is beautiful in its own class. It adorns earthly darkness and is useful at night; for all of these reasons it deserves praise in its own small way. How then can he properly say that the moon should not exist, when he would laugh at himself for saying that lamps should not exist? But perhaps, instead of saying that the moon should not exist at all, he would say that the moon ought to be as bright as the sun. This amounts to saying: 'the moon should not exist, but there should be two suns.' In this way he makes two mistakes: by desiring another sun, he tries to add to the perfection of creation; and by wanting to take away the moon, he tries to weaken that perfection.

When you observe the differences among material objects and see that some are brighter than others, it would be wrong to want to get rid of the darker ones, or to make them just like the brighter ones. Instead, if you refer all of them to the perfection of the whole, you will see that these differences in brightness contribute to the more perfect being of the universe. The universe would not be perfect unless the greater things were present in such a way that lesser things are not excluded. In the same way, when you consider the differences among souls, you will find that the unhappiness that grieves you also contributes to the perfection of the whole by ensuring that it includes even those souls who deserved to be made unhappy because they willed to be sinners. God was perfectly justified in making such

souls, just as he deserves praise for making other creatures that
are far inferior even to unhappy souls.

In this passage, Augustine transforms Plato's assumption
about divine perfection from part of the problem to part of the
solution. The explanation behind the puzzling phenomenon of
evil is that it ultimately contributes to the perfection of the
universe.

Augustine bases his argument on a running analogy about the
sun and the moon. An **argument from analogy** can be
dissected using the following schema:

1. A is to B as C is to D.
2. A is P with respect to B.

---

3. Therefore, C is P with respect to D.

Although this schema is deductively valid, it is also somewhat circular in so far as premise (1) alone is virtually equivalent
to the conclusion. Nevertheless, by reconstructing the argument
in this way we can at least see exactly what the author is saying.

In this case, Augustine's argument can be reconstructed as
follows:

1. The sun is to the moon as happy souls are to unhappy
souls.
2. The sun would not occupy a perfect universe without the
moon.

---

3. Therefore happy souls would not occupy a perfect
universe without unhappy souls.

A perfect universe requires both happiness and unhappiness.

Notice the crucial appearance of the great chain of being
once again in this passage. Augustine is relying on the thesis that
degrees of goodness are required for perfection. Does this seem
true? Consider a counterexample – such as an Olympic gymnastic
floor routine. What does the gymnast need to do to earn a

perfect score? Surely including moves that are not as good will spoil a perfect score.

Augustine might respond to this objection by pointing out that a perfect gymnastic floor routine does include both greater and lesser things. The gymnast's first somersault could be performed by any amateur while her final double-twisting front flip could only be performed by a highly trained professional. Just because the somersault is a lesser good than the flip doesn't mean it's imperfect. On the contrary, lesser goods are required to complement the greater goods.

This objection and response show that Augustine can maintain a consistent position provided he is prepared to embrace the rather unintuitive thesis that unhappiness isn't a really a bad thing.

Augustine's defence of God

Augustine returned to the problem of suffering many times throughout the course of his career as though he himself was never completely satisfied with his solution. In the passage below from a work called *Catechism on Faith, Hope, and Love*, he tries to answer the following question: In creating sinners, is God responsible for evil?

EVIL IS NOT A THING

All things are created by God and everything created by God is good. So then what is that which we call 'evil'? In the bodies of animals, 'disease' and 'wound' signify the absence of health. For when the animal is cured, the disease or wound doesn't go away and exist elsewhere. The flesh of the animal is a substance. The wound or disease is not itself a substance but a defect in the substance. In the same way, the soul of a human being is a substance, while a vice is a defect in the soul. This is evident in that when vices leave the soul, they cannot exist anywhere else. Since evil is not a substance but a defect in a substance it is not created by God.

All things that exist, therefore, are themselves good, seeing that the Creator of them all is supremely good. But because they are not, like their Creator, supremely and unchangeably good, their good may be diminished and increased. Evil is the disintegration of goodness. Goodness can only disintegrate so much without ceasing to exist altogether. For regardless of what kind of being we are talking about, its goodness cannot be destroyed without destroying the being itself. The reason is that goodness is being, and being is goodness.

An uncorrupted nature is justly admired. Moreover, if it be incorruptible, it is undoubtedly even more valuable. When it is corrupted, however, its corruption is an evil, because it is deprived of some of its good. If it be deprived of no good, then it has received no injury; but if it has received injury, then it is deprived of some good. Therefore, so long as a being is in process of corruption, there is in it some good of which it is being deprived. If a part of the being should remain which cannot be corrupted, this will certainly be an incorruptible being. Accordingly, the process of corruption will result in the manifestation of this great good. But if it should be thoroughly and completely consumed by corruption, there will then be no good left, because there will be no being. Corruption can consume the good only by consuming the being.

Every being, therefore, is a good – a great good if it can't be corrupted, a lesser good if it can. In any case, only a fool or an idiot will deny that it is a good. And if it be wholly consumed by corruption, then the corruption itself must cease to exist, as there is no being left in which it can dwell.

In this passage Augustine asserts that God doesn't create evil because he only creates beings and evil is not a being but rather a lack of being.

The first thing to note is that this passage echoes the same belligerent tone of the last passage. At the end of this passage Augustine declares that 'only a fool or an idiot' would deny what he is saying. Likewise, in the last passage, Augustine says it would be 'wicked and spiteful' to take the view he opposes.

In the last chapter we saw that Anselm refers to his opponent as 'the fool.' While Anselm's use of this pejorative term can be excused as an allusion to the Bible, Augustine's pejoratives are plausibly interpreted as instances of the **fallacy** 'ad hominem.' **Ad hominem**, which is Latin for 'against the man,' occurs when the author tries to win the argument by discrediting the character or reputation of his opponent. It is akin to mudslinging in politics. As Bishop of Hippo, Augustine was pressured into a great deal of political wrangling, so it is not surprising to see him resorting to such tactics from time to time.

Setting this aside, however, we see that, once again, Augustine relies on an analogy to make his case: Disease is to the body as evil is to the soul. Disease is a name for the body's disintegration. Therefore, evil is a name for the soul's disintegration.

Augustine proceeds to reason by modus tollens as follows:

1. One is responsible for something only if one made it.
2. God did not make evil.

---

3. Therefore, God is not responsible for evil.

(Notice that 'P only if Q' means 'If P then Q.' It does not mean 'If Q then P' even though the 'if' occurs before Q.)

Is premise (1) plausible? Do we hold human beings responsible only for what they make or do we also hold them responsible for what they fail to make? We can use another analogy to explore this question.

Suppose you have invited a houseful of people over for dinner. You work in the kitchen all day to make a gourmet chicken dish. Your guests gobble it up. The only problem is that, because you didn't cook the chicken long enough, it gives them salmonella. Soon they all grow very sick and one even dies. Would you feel bad, or would you feel that you should be given credit for the large amount of cooking you did, rather than blamed for the small amount you didn't do? Suppose further that the family of the dead guest eventually sues you for the medical bills and for the pain and trauma they suffered as a result of your undercooked dinner. Would it make sense to argue that you can't be held responsible for a lack of cooking? Hardly.

Augustine might respond to this objection by insisting that there is a disanalogy between God's universe and your dinner. In the case of your dinner, it is both possible and expected that no one will be poisoned. It is not clear, however, that either such a possibility or such an expectation applies to God's universe. First, Augustine might deny the possibility of an evil-free universe as follows: Given that God must create perfection, that perfection requires both greater and lesser degrees of goodness, and that lesser degrees of goodness allow evil, God must allow evil. Second, Augustine might deny that it is reasonable to have any expectation of God. Because God is infinitely wiser than we are, he may have reason for allowing evil that we can't understand. Or he simply may not owe us any reason.

There is another problem with Augustine's comparison between disease and evil, however. A disease is something that happens to a person while evil is something that a person can make happen.

Consider cancer, a classic example of disease. It is typically caused by a genetic predisposition and/or an environmental contaminant. A person who has cancer is regarded as a victim – and hopefully a survivor – of a terrible blow. We don't typically blame cancer patients for getting cancer. We may blame a man who gets lung cancer after smoking for many years, provided he knew the risk. But we also recognize that smoking is an addiction that is extremely difficult to break. We are more likely to feel sorry for him.

Now consider date rape, a classic example of evil. Typical cases of date rape involve a man forcing sex on a woman he knows, often with the help of threats or drugs. We don't typically regard a date rapist as a victim at all. On the contrary, he is the victimizer. We typically blame him for making a very bad choice and we don't feel sorry for him even if he has trouble with regular dating.

By comparing evil to a disease, Augustine suggests that human beings can't help it that their souls are corrupted. Nor is this just a misleading result of one analogy. Elsewhere in his work, Augustine begins to see the bad choices people make as a product of what he calls 'ignorance and difficulty.' Ignorance is when you don't know the right thing to do and difficulty is when you can't get yourself to do the right thing even when you know what it is. In light of this handicap it is no wonder that human beings are sinners! While this does a lot to explain the sad state of the world it also destroys choice. Although Augustine continued all his life to profess belief in free will, many of his readers find his position to be inconsistent with it. Some later medieval philosophers saw fit to correct Augustine on this issue.

Olivi's libertarianism

Metaphysical libertarianism is the view that human beings are responsible for their actions as individuals because they have free will, defined as the ability to choose in such a way that they could have chosen otherwise. Metaphysical libertarianism is opposed to **determinism**, according to which human beings do not have free will but rather are determined by antecedent conditions (such as God or nature or environmental factors) to choose one way as opposed to another.

Suppose Jake eats a cupcake. According to the determinist,

antecedent conditions caused him to do this. Hence, he could not have done otherwise unless those antecedent conditions had been different. Given the same conditions, Jake cannot refrain from eating the cupcake. Determinists are content to conclude that freedom is an illusion.

Compatibilism is a version of determinism according to which being determined to do exactly what we do is compatible with freedom as long as the antecedent conditions that determine what we do include our own choices. Compatibilists claim that the choices we make are free even though we could not do otherwise given the same antecedent conditions. On this view, Jake chose to eat the cupcake because his desire for it outweighed all other considerations at that moment. Our choices are always determined by our strongest desires according to compatibilists.

Metaphysical libertarians reject determinism and compatibilism, insisting that free will includes the ability to act against our strongest desires. On this view, Jake could have refrained from eating the cupcake even given the exact same antecedent conditions. While desires influence our choices they do not cause our choices according to metaphysical libertarianism; rather, our choices are caused by our will which is itself an uncaused cause, meaning that it is an independent power, stronger than any antecedent condition. This notion of free will enables the metaphysical libertarian to assign a very strong conception of individual responsibility to human beings: what we do is not attributable to God or nature or environmental factors.

The first philosopher ever to make a clear case for metaphysical libertarianism was Peter John Olivi. Olivi claims to love Augustine and hate Aristotle. Nevertheless, he is convinced that Augustine has wandered too far away from free will in his investigation of the problem of suffering. In the passage that follows, Olivi turns to empiricism to restore human freedom to its pure form.

FREE WILL IS OBSERVABLE

We observe the freedom of the will through internal experience. When there is some number of equal things that are equally useful, nothing explains the will's adoption of one or the other of them except the freedom by which one is equally able to do this or that. Suppose there are two pieces of fruit or two people that are in every way and through all things similar and equivalent. Nevertheless, the will attaches itself to one of the two and leaves the other.

It might be objected that the same can be said of animals when they choose one of two things that are equally desirable and equally distant from them. But it is evident that the cases are not similar, because animals do not deliberate over the equality of the choice nor even do they make a judgment as a human being does.

It often happens that we want to take one of two coins. We deliberate and ascertain that there is just as good reason to take the one as the other. In these circumstances, we rightly think that we would be able to take and keep the one coin just as well as the other. Then, when we take one of the two, we manifestly feel that we do this from freedom of the will alone and not from some greater satisfaction in the one as opposed to the other.

The objector might persist, however: what then determines the appetite of an animal to one object rather than the other?

Although it is difficult to give a good explanation, it can be said that the appetite and the senses of the animal are in continual motion or in continual agitation as if pushed along continuously by nature. Under these circumstances it is hardly possible for the momentum to be uniform in every way. For this reason the animal's apprehension of and appetite for the object easily varies. It will always find one object more satisfying or perhaps more easily attainable than the other.

The act of the will, in contrast, is entirely indeterminate. Suppose at the moment of acting you are inclined toward your act in the same way animals are inclined toward theirs. Then, as you begin to act, you would not feel in you a certain power not to do that which you are doing. Everyone undeniably feels within themselves a certain power that is not determined. Hence, when he does something, he is able not to do it and when he does not do something, he is able to do it.

For Olivi, the knowledge of free will comes from within. Nevertheless, we wouldn't consider this an innatist proof because it relies on observation rather than reason. According to empiricists, knowledge comes from observation of the world. Olivi is suggesting that the working of the mind is part of the world that can be observed.

Olivi's argument can be reconstructed using modus tollens as follows:

1. If human beings weren't free, then, when we are about to do something, we wouldn't feel like we are able not to do it.

2. When we are about to do something we do feel like we are able not to do it.

---

3. Therefore, human beings are free.

Olivi uses the empirical examples of choosing between equivalent pieces of fruit, people, or coins in order to support premise (2). He invites his readers to consult their own experience and see whether it is true that they feel like they could select one or the other of the two. This argument for libertarianism has come to be known as the **argument from introspection** and it has been repeated many times throughout the history of philosophy.

Olivi uses examples of selecting between equivalent options because he believes this is when free will is most readily apparent. The example of selecting between a coin and a cockroach would not illustrate free will very well because most people would be strongly inclined away from the roach and toward the coin. Olivi is happy to grant that sometimes our inclinations are sufficient to cause our actions without any free will. In such cases, he says, we are 'dragged into action.' He further asserts that animals are always determined in this way. But human beings have the power of thought, which enables us to deliberate. In cases where our inclinations are not overpowering, free will enables us to go either way.

It's hard to deny premise (2). Most people do feel that in cases of deliberation they could go either way. Premise (1), however, is highly controversial. Is it true that we wouldn't feel this way unless we were free? That is, could there be some other

PETER JOHN OLIVI 1248–1298

Peter John Olivi joined the Franciscan monastic order, or 'Order of the Friars Minor,' O.F.M., at the age of twelve. He went on to earn his degree at the University of Paris.

While distinguishing himself as a teacher and as a writer, he soon became involved in a controversy concerning the Franciscan vow of poverty. Some argued for a relaxed interpretation of the vow; others argued for a rigorous interpretation. Olivi was a rigorist. Unfortunately for him, the Church authorities were on the opposite side. After an official investigation, he was accused of heresy and his works were confiscated.

Because Olivi was able to defend himself, his reputation was restored and he was allowed to teach again. He died in good standing with the Church. After his death, however, the same controversy flared up, worse than before. Olivi's works were burned and his tomb desecrated.

Despite the official ban on Olivi, many philosophers continued to read his work *sub rosa*. Direct influence is evident on his fellow Franciscans, John Duns Scotus and William of Ockham. Although Olivi contributed some of the most original ideas of the late middle ages, he was of necessity unacknowledged.

explanation for why deliberation makes us feel as though we could go either way?

Buridan's ass

By the fourteenth century, some philosophers were content to defend compatibilism and even determinism, giving up on free will even if they still paid lip service to it. Jean Buridan offers an account of deliberation that explains the feeling of indeterminacy without any reliance on free will.

In Buridan's view, the will is nothing other than another name for the intellect. The intellect is responsible for moving human beings into deliberate action and it is always motivated by reasons. If two options present themselves, there will always be reasons for each. The intellect's job is to select whichever option is attached to the best reasons. When things go smoothly we don't ever feel the moment of hesitation that Olivi considers the mark of free will.

Things rarely go smoothly, however, due to desire. Suppose you are trying to decide how to spend the rest of the afternoon. You could do an exercise workout, or you could watch a re-run of your favourite television show. You have all kinds of good reasons to do the workout and almost no good reason to watch TV. Nevertheless, you want to watch TV and you don't want to do your workout. So you put off the decision for a little while 'in order to decide.' Soon someone in your house turns the TV on, and before long you are watching your show, having forgotten all about the idea of doing a workout. By postponing the decision and distracting our attention, desire can free us from the dictates of reason. So the illusion of free will is really nothing other than defective reasoning.

Olivi and his followers found this account of human freedom entirely inadequate. One of them, though it remains a mystery exactly who, proposed a thought experiment to demonstrate the absurdity of Buridan's view. It has come to be known as **Buridan's ass**.

Imagine a hungry donkey placed at equal distances between two equally appealing piles of hay. The donkey has reason to approach a pile of hay but does not have reason to approach one pile as opposed to the other. For lack of ability to break the tie, the donkey starves to death. In so doing, the donkey is supposed to vindicate the special dignity of being human. Placed in a similar situation, we would not starve. Our free will enables us to break a tie without a reason.

Note that a **thought experiment** is a fictional scenario designed to test our intuitions about a controversial claim. It won't do to object that a donkey could never get into such a fix in real life. The point of the scenario is to provide a fictional illustration of what the hypothesis of free will is intended to accomplish. No doubt today we would change Buridan's ass to Buridan's computer: What happens when you program a computer with conflicting instructions? The program comes to a complete halt – it may even shut down. Human beings, in contrast, can cope quite easily with conflicting instructions – we can choose.

Olivi is bent on establishing this point because he thinks it is necessary for moral responsibility. In his view, it is as though we have a devil sitting on one shoulder and an angel sitting on the other. Each is whispering in our ear. Although the instructions from the devil and the angel are completely different from each other we feel torn between them. The devil and the angel provide equally compelling reasons, though one set is bad and the other set is good. Olivi insists that we can only be held responsible for our choice if we are fully aware of and able to follow either one. Neither Buridan nor Augustine allows for this.

In the following passage, Olivi explains the difference between a human being and an ass.

FREE WILL IS NECESSARY FOR VIRTUE AND VICE

The act of willing must be indeterminate since it can be good or evil, virtuous or vicious. Some say that an act of willing is of itself determined toward virtue and that vice does not happen unless sensual desire blocks reason. But this is not plausible. For an action happens either naturally or freely. If it happens naturally, then it is not vicious because it was dragged toward evil necessarily. In this case we would have to attribute vice to sensuality rather than to the will. But who would say that immoderate appetite, inordinate desire for wealth and glory, or hatred of good people and even God do not come from the will but only from the violent yanking of sensuality? If, on the other hand, the will is indeterminate to good and bad action, equally susceptible to virtue and vice, then the determination can be given neither by the object nor by sensuality, at least not in any necessary way. Therefore, the will must have the determination from itself. But it cannot have such determination unless it has the free power to do one thing or the other.

It is evident, therefore, that the error of determinism destroys every good of human beings and God while permitting every crime and misdeed. Nor is this any wonder, since, as I have shown, it reduces us to nothing more than intellectual beasts.

In Olivi's view, it would be unjust for God to punish human beings if we can't help being sinners.

Of course, compatibilists and determinists have other ways of explaining moral responsibility. They would insist that it is fair to hold someone responsible for doing evil even if they can't help it. Consider the compulsive shoplifter. Just because she can't help stealing doesn't mean we should let her continue to do it. She has to be stopped and a stiff penalty might actually help her curb her compulsion. This is a **reformatory conception of justice**, according to which the purpose of punishment is to prevent future wrongdoing. Compatibilists and determinists might claim that it is more humane to regard wrongdoing as a consequence of circumstances rather than free will.

There are, however, problems with reformative justice. The shoplifter may take so much pleasure in stealing that no punishment will stop her. Or she may continue to believe that she will get away with it the next time. Furthermore, with more serious crimes like murder, once is enough to ruin the lives of everyone involved. In a crime of passion, repeated offence may not even be an issue.

Metaphysical libertarians seem to be holding out for a **retributive conception of justice**, according to which the purpose of punishment is to make the criminal pay for the crime. No matter how dire the circumstances, the criminal could have chosen otherwise. Hence we are justified in feeling blame toward those who choose badly and admiration toward those who choose well. Metaphysical libertarians might claim that on the compatibilist/determinist view no one can really take credit for anything.

The main problem with retributive justice is that it is closely related to revenge, which is typically regarded as a vice. Many would argue that it is better to cultivate an attitude of forgiveness than to focus on exacting an eye for an eye and a tooth for a tooth.

The debate over free will continues and its connection to the problem of suffering further complicates it. Prima facie, it looks as though free will is necessary to explain the suffering we see around us. On further examination, however, it becomes clear that there is far more suffering than free will could ever account for. Why would God allow it? Augustine asserts that he allows it as punishment for our sins. But if our sins are the result of our defective nature, then it seems we are not to blame. So it is hard to maintain both that God is just and that responsibility requires free will.

4
Eternity

There is no yesterday nor any tomorrow,
but only *now*, as it was a thousand years ago
and as it will be a thousand years hence.

Meister Eckhart

In the previous two chapters we saw how 'all-powerful,' 'all-knowing,' and 'all-loving' are crucial characteristics of God. If God lacked one of these characteristics he would not be the supreme being in the universe. The term 'eternal' is typically taken to mean 'staying the same forever.' This is another crucial characteristic for God. If God exists, then he has always existed and will always exist unchanged. He doesn't go through birth, growth, and death like the rest of us because these changes make us fragile and imperfect. But Christians were calling God 'eternal' long before anyone ever worked out just what this means.

The divine idleness question

Although Christianity took a strong hold in the Mediterranean region by AD 400, many Roman citizens were still pagans. Roman pagans worshipped many gods and goddesses such as Jupiter, Juno, Mars, and Venus. Because they were a lot like humans, these gods and goddesses were easier to understand than the Christian God. They were born and had physical bodies. They interacted directly with humans in real time. Although they didn't often die, they could get hurt and they had limited powers.

One of the most difficult things for pagans to understand about the Christian God was how he could have existed in complete perfection from all eternity. When Augustine became bishop of Hippo, they taunted him with impossible questions about God's eternal nature. 'If God has existed forever,' they wanted to know, 'what was he doing all by himself for all that while before he created the universe?' This is known as the **divine idleness question**.

Although this may seem like a silly question, it's actually very serious because it exposes the problem of how a changeless being could be related to a changing world.

In order to answer it, Augustine makes a classic philosophical move – he steps back to question the question. Does such a question have an answer? Generally speaking, philosophers celebrate difficult questions. It is their trademark to deal with questions that other people don't dare even to ask. Nevertheless, some questions cannot be answered due to logical difficulties.

Consider the following question: 'What is the opposite of a bird?' This question commits what philosophers call a 'category mistake.' A **category mistake** occurs when a sentence makes an impossible presupposition about its subject. The question under consideration presupposes that a bird is the kind of thing that can have an opposite, but it isn't. Direction is a category that has opposites. For example, up is the opposite of down and in is the opposite of out. Birds are not like directions. Their category, 'animal,' doesn't have opposites. So the question doesn't make any sense. In philosophical terms, the question is logically incoherent. (The term 'incoherent' comes from the Latin words for 'doesn't stick together.')

Augustine tackles the following question: Is the question, 'What was God doing before he created the universe?' coherent? His answer to this question is found in the following passage from book 11 of the *Confessions*.

THERE WAS NO TIME BEFORE TIME

Here's a deep question: 'What was God doing before he made heaven and earth?' I might answer, 'He was preparing hell for those who ask deep questions.' Ha ha! But no – I'm not going to shrug this one off with a joke. I'd rather admit I don't know the answer than ridicule a deep question.

One thing is certain: God is the creator of everything. So, if the term 'heaven and earth' means everything, then we know the answer to the question. God didn't make anything before he made heaven and earth. For what could he make but some *thing* – which would constitute part of heaven and earth? If I know one thing for sure it's that God can't make something before he starts making things.

But suppose someone was pondering the very beginning and seriously began to wonder what you, the almighty God, were doing with yourself all that time before you suddenly decided to create the world. Well, in my view, thinking about a time before the creation of the world is an illusion. After all, what age could exist before the beginning of the ages? How could there be periods of time that were not made by you? If they weren't made by you then they didn't exist because you are the creator of all things.

Suppose there was time before you made heaven and earth. Then it's not as though you were just sitting around during that time. On the contrary, you must have been busy making time itself. Periods could not pass by until you made the whole temporal procession.

Suppose, on the other hand, there was no time before you made heaven and earth. Then we can't even ask, 'What were you doing then?' For there was no 'then' when there was no time!

There was no time, therefore, when you had not made anything, because you made time itself. This doesn't mean that times are co-eternal with you. When we say you are eternal we mean that you stay the same forever; but if times stayed the same forever, then they wouldn't be times.

Again, the question is, 'What did God make before he made heaven and earth?' We are far out of our depth when we try to answer such a question! Worse yet is the question, 'How did it come into God's mind to make something, when he never made anything before?' I'm going to try to hold steadfastly to the truth on this issue, O Lord. The trick is to see that you can't speak of 'never' where there is no time. Something can't suddenly 'come into God's mind' when God is forever unchanging. We should therefore stop blabbering in vain! There could be no time without the existence of a created being because time itself is a created being. As the eternal creator of all times, you are metaphysically prior to all times and no time can be co-eternal with you.

Augustine makes it clear in this passage that he thinks the question under consideration is incoherent.

As always, there are a number of ways to interpret his argument. We can focus on the third paragraph, where he says 'Well, in my view, thinking about a time before the creation of the world is an illusion. After all, what age could exist before the beginning of the ages?' We can reconstruct this reasoning using an extended form of modus tollens as follows:

1. If a question is answerable, then it must not presuppose an impossibility.

2. The question 'What was God doing before he created the world?' presupposes that there was an age before the beginning of the ages.

3. It is impossible for there to be an age before the beginning of the ages.

---

4. Therefore, the question, 'What was God doing before he created the world?' is not answerable.

This argument is valid. Is it sound?

One might object to premise (2) by insisting that the question actually presupposes two different senses of the word 'age.' Suppose we restate the presupposition as follows: There was a heavenly age before the beginning of the earthly age. Then we avoid the problem. In fact, Augustine himself alludes to such a possibility in the fourth paragraph when he says, 'suppose there was time before you made heaven and earth. Then it's not as though you were just sitting around during that time. On the contrary, you must have been busy making time itself.' As long as we are talking about two different kinds of age, there is no contradiction in saying that one existed before the beginning of the other.

Augustine could easily respond to this objection, however, by pointing out that it just pushes the same question back a step. We can now ask, 'What was God doing before he created the heavenly age?' This response is designed to show that the objection is mired in the same contradiction as the original question: that there was an age before the beginning of ages. If there was a third kind of age that came before the heavenly age, then there could be a fourth kind of age that came before the third (and so on, and so on, ad infinitum). This result seems to confirm the absurdity of the original question.

Augustine's view of the nature of time

Having clarified God's relationship to time, Augustine moves on to consider the nature of time itself. The question he lays out for consideration is this: Does time exist objectively or is time a subjective feature of our minds?

Some argue that the past, present, and future coexist in a fourth dimension beyond human experience. On this view, there is no such thing as real change. Change is an illusion we experience due to the fact that we have to experience time moment by moment in successive order. We can call this view **temporal realism**, meaning that time exists independently of the way the human mind experiences it.

The opposing view is **temporal anti-realism**, meaning that time is dependent on the human mind. On this view, neither the past nor the future exists except in our minds. The past is nothing but a memory and the future is nothing but an expectation. Even the present is nothing but a constantly changing awareness.

In the passage below, also from book 11 of the *Confessions*, Augustine takes a stand on this issue.

THE NATURE OF TIME

What is time? Who can explain it? Who can comprehend it or put the answer into words? Yet we constantly refer to it in conversation. And we seem to understand it when we refer to it or when we hear someone else refer to it.

What, then, is time? If no one asks me, I know what it is. But the minute I try to explain, it escapes me.

Yet I will boldly assert that if nothing passed away, the past would not exist, and if nothing were coming, the future would not exist, and if nothing were, then the present would not exist. Those two times then, past and future, how do they exist, considering that the past now is not, and that the future is not yet? And what about the present? If it were always present, and never passed away, it would not be time, but eternity. The present, if it exists, comes into existence only as it passes out of existence! How can we affirm the existence of something whose cause of being is not being?

It is in our minds that we feel and measure the length of time. Let us see then whether the present can be long. Are a hundred years, when present, a long time? See first, whether a hundred years can be present. If the first of these years is now present, then the other ninety-nine are future, and therefore do not yet exist. Likewise, if the second year is present, then one is now past and the rest future. Likewise, if we assume any middle year of this hundred to be present, all before it are past, all after it, future. Therefore, a hundred years cannot be present.

But let's see at least whether that one year, which is now current, can be present. If the first month is current, the rest are future. If the second is current, the first is already past and the rest are future. Therefore, we can't say that the current year is present either! And if the year cannot be present as a whole then it cannot be present at all.

So, the present time, which alone can be called 'long,' is abridged to the length of one day. But let us examine this also because neither is one day present as a whole. For it is made up of twenty-four hours. The first has the rest in the future, the last has them in the past, and any of the middle has those before it past, those behind it in the future. Help! Even one hour passes away in flying particles. The part of it that has flown away is past. The part of it that remains is future.

Suppose we conceive of an instant of time that cannot be divided into the smallest particles of moments and call it alone 'the present.' Still, it flies with such speed from future to past, as not to stay for any length. For, if it stays for any length, then we can divide it into past and future.

The present has no space. Where then is time, which we may call 'long'?

It's clearly incorrect to say that there are three times – past, present, and future. Instead it seems more accurate to say that there are three present times – a time present of things past; a time present of things present; and a time present of things future. These three do coexist somehow in the mind, for otherwise I could not see them. The time present of things past is memory; the time present of things present is direct experience; the time present of things future is expectation. So, time is in the mind.

In this passage, Augustine advocates temporal anti-realism. He is arguing that if time existed objectively outside our minds, it would have to have some length. He then sets out to see whether he can show that it has length. Upon failing to accomplish this he concludes that time must not exist outside the mind.

Augustine's reasoning can be reconstructed in *reductio ad absurdum* form as follows:

To prove: Time exists only in the mind.

1. Suppose time exists outside the mind.

2. If time exists outside the mind then it must have length.

3. If time has length then the present must have length.

4. If the present must have length then a single instant must have length.

5. But a single instant with length is impossible.

---

6. Therefore, time exists only in the mind.

Although this argument is valid, its soundness is controversial.

What does it mean to say that time exists only in the mind? This may seem like a very naïve, old-fashioned view. Surely modern science has overturned Augustine's temporal anti-realism and established that time is an objectively existing external reality?

It is true that the dominant view among scientists today is temporal realism, that time is an objectively existing external reality. However, it is important to realize that this is an assumption scientists make in order to construct efficient formulas; they have not proven it to be true. In fact, there is good reason to question temporal realism due to various anomalies in the formulas that describe the laws of the universe. For example, when astrophysicists try to describe the state of the universe shortly after the big bang, temporal variables cease to make sense. This suggests that these temporal variables may just be convenient approximations for typical conditions rather than accurate measurements of reality itself.

Still, some might accuse Augustine of falling victim in this passage to a category mistake just like the one he handily sidestepped in the last passage. Does the question 'What is time?' make sense?

Consider by comparison the question 'What is a colour'? The answer is that a colour is a visual characteristic of things that results from light emitted or reflected. Now consider the question 'What is yellow?' If someone asked you this question, how would you answer it? You might say it is one of the three primary colours. But this doesn't narrow it down very well at all. You're more apt to point to a clear instance of yellow, such as an egg yolk or a canary. But physical objects can only convey particular shades of yellow. No single object or collection of objects can define yellow itself. Perhaps you might try to stipulate the wavelengths of light that fall within the range of yellow. But wavelengths of light do not constitute colour without a perceiver. After all, a colour-blind perceiver might see those very same wavelengths as a completely different colour.

In short, the question 'What is ——?' seems to presuppose that whatever is inserted in the blank should be a kind of thing. Kinds of things have definitions. Although a kiss is a kind of thing, love is not. Not surprisingly, therefore, the question 'What is love?' is equally perplexing. Time, like yellow and love, is not a kind of thing but an experience. Under these circumstances perhaps Augustine should have rejected the question as unanswerable.

On the other hand, if it is true that the question 'What is time?' is unanswerable because it is an experience like love or yellow, then this ultimately reinforces Augustine's conclusion. Yellow and love occur within the mind and would not exist if there were no conscious minds to experience them. This is exactly what anti-realism asserts about time. So it looks like Augustine may have been correct to defend this view after all.

By defending temporal anti-realism, the view that time is just a feature of the human mind, Augustine solved some problems. At the same time, however, he raised a host of other questions for his successors to try to answer.

The problem of divine foreknowledge

Boethius was born a few generations after Augustine died. Reading Augustine as well as Plato and Aristotle, he became interested in how God knows the future. Divine foreknowledge is a puzzle that continues to exercise the minds of philosophers who believe in God.

BOETHIUS c. 475–526

Boethius was born into a wealthy political family in Rome and received the best education available, with training in both Latin and Greek literature. He became chief magistrate of the Roman senate while only in his mid-twenties.

Because his senatorial position was mostly no more than an honorific title, Boethius was able to spend much of his time doing what he loved, namely, philosophy. He was also happily married with several children. Trouble, however, was on the way.

When Boethius was in his mid-forties, Theodoric, the king of the Germanic tribe that was then ruling half of the former Roman Empire, appointed him as a top-level assistant at his royal court. Soon one of Boethius's fellow senators was arrested by Theodoric under suspicion of conspiracy. Boethius defended the suspect and thereby instantly became *persona non grata*.

Theodoric imprisoned Boethius in peasant quarters for one year while he decided what to do about the situation. The end must have come as a shock to everyone. Boethius was convicted of treason without a fair trial, tortured, and executed.

As we have already seen, God is supposed to be omniscient, meaning that he knows absolutely everything there is to be known. Foreknowledge is a crucial aspect of God's omniscience. If God didn't know how the future was going to go then he wouldn't be able to reveal prophesies or guarantee his promises, as indicated in the Bible. If he had to wait to find out what happens like the rest of us, then good may not triumph over evil in the end.

Boethius became interested in divine foreknowledge because of the tragic circumstances of his life. He was a very happy and successful man until one day the king arrested him and put him in prison for a crime he did not commit. He had to wait in prison for a year to find out whether he would be set free or executed. What a miserable year it was! Boethius passed the time by writing a book called *The Consolation of Philosophy*. Combining poetry and prose, this book explores philosophical questions about luck, fate, freedom, and God. Boethius wrote in the form of a dialogue between himself and 'Lady Philosophy,' a female character he invented to represent the combined wisdom of Plato and Aristotle.

The most famous section of the book raises the question: how can God know the future without destroying human freedom? This question, known as the **problem of divine foreknowledge**, becomes especially vivid when you consider Boethius's situation. Today he sits in prison. Tomorrow the king will decide whether he lives or dies. The king is free to decide either way. Yet God already knows exactly what he will decide. If God already knows what the king will decide, how can the king be free to decide either way? It seems God's foreknowledge proves there really is no such thing as human freedom.

Boethius presents his concern to Lady Philosophy in the following passage of *The Consolation of Philosophy*.

THE CONFLICT BETWEEN FOREKNOWLEDGE AND FREE WILL

There seems to me to be a severe incompatibility between God's foreknowledge of the future and human free will. If God foresees all things and cannot be mistaken about anything, then whatever he foresees must happen. So, if he knows beforehand, not only people's deeds but even their plans and wishes, there will be no freedom of judgment. After all, no deed can be done and no wish can be formed except exactly as the infallible mind of God has foreseen. If matters could be overturned so that they resulted otherwise than was foreseen by God, then his foreknowledge would cease to be certain. Rather than knowledge, it would be mere opinion, which is uncertain and unsuitable for God.

I don't agree with some people who think they can solve this problem by saying that a thing is not going to happen because God has foreseen it but rather that God has foreseen it because it is going to happen. They say it is not necessary for the thing that was foreseen to happen. Instead, it is necessary for the thing that happens to be foreseen. They insist that the entire solution lies in showing that the thing happening causes the foreknowledge rather than the foreknowledge causing the thing to happen.

I argue, however, that it makes absolutely no difference which causes which. Either way, the outcome is the same: the foreknowledge makes the future happening necessary. Suppose a man sits, and you hold the true opinion that this man is sitting. Well, then he must be sitting. He does not sit because your opinion about him is true. Rather, your opinion about him is true because he is sitting. Nevertheless, the truth of your opinion guarantees that he is sitting. Likewise, I grant that future events don't happen because of God's foreknowledge. Yet his foreknowledge guarantees that they will happen, which is alone enough to destroy the freedom of the will.

In this passage Boethius criticises a common answer to the question he has raised.

The common answer goes like this: Just because God *knows* the king's future decision doesn't mean he *causes* the king's future decision. That's not how knowledge works, as we see in the ordinary case of human knowledge. If you see a man sitting down then you know he is sitting down. But your knowing this does not cause it to happen. So why would we think that God's knowing the king's decision causes the king's decision?

Boethius complains that this answer to his question entirely misses the point. He never worried that God is *causing* the king's decision. On the contrary, he worried that God *guarantees* the decision without causing it. Suppose the king freely makes his own decision tomorrow to execute Boethius. The problem is that God already knows about that decision today, and in fact has always known about it, even before the king was ever born. So how could the king have decided to do the opposite? His ability to set Boethius free instead would be an ability to prove God wrong, which is impossible.

When people who believe in God hear this way of stating the problem, they generally grant that God always knew that the king would decide to execute Boethius. They insist, however, that this doesn't affect the king's freedom because the king himself didn't know what he was going to decide. On this view, it doesn't matter that God already knows the entire future. As long as *we* don't know it, we are free.

This response to the problem, however, is entirely indefensible. Not knowing what you will decide is not the same as being free to decide. In fact, if our freedom consists in ignorance alone, then it is a sham.

We can prove that freedom requires more than ignorance with a simple example. Suppose you have agreed to take your five-year-old niece to the movies. When you arrive to pick her up you tell her that there are two different movies starting in one hour and that she gets to decide which one of them the two of you will go to. She is thrilled that you regard her as grown up enough to make the decision. She spends the hour thinking carefully about it, changing her mind several times, and asking her friends for advice. Little does she know that you already bought tickets to one of the movies and will see to it that this is what she 'decides.'

Most people will agree that this is a manipulative and deceitful way of treating someone. If you tell someone that she gets to decide, then you have to be prepared to go either way. It is bad enough to fool one child this way on one occasion; it would be far worse for God to fool all of us this way all of the time. If he really has given us freedom to decide, then this doesn't just mean that we don't know which way our decisions will go. It means our decisions could really go either way.

The reason God's knowledge of the future seems to take away our freedom is because God's knowledge of the future can't be wrong. This is different from human knowledge.

For example, human beings have become pretty good at predicting the weather. Suppose a first-rate meteorologist predicts that a tornado will strike a certain place at a certain time tomorrow and it happens exactly as she predicted. Then we say that she knew it all along. Does that mean that there was no way for the tornado to go a different direction instead? No. The reason is that human knowledge is fallible. The meteorologist knew exactly where and when the tornado would strike, but she could have been wrong.

God's knowledge, in contrast, is not fallible. It is never the case that he could have been wrong. So everything has to go exactly as he foresees it, including our decisions. How therefore can we be free?

The sceptic will conclude that we can't be free under these circumstances. We can capture the sceptic's view in the following argument:

1. If we are free, then our future decisions can go either way.

2. If our future decisions can go either way, then God can't now know which way they will go.

_____

3. Therefore, if we are free, then God can't now know which way our future decisions will go.

This argument uses hypothetical syllogism to generate a dilemma. If you accept the premises, then you have to give up either human free will or divine foreknowledge.

Boethius's solution

Although Boethius articulates the sceptic's position with conviction, he ultimately wants to refute it. After some deeper investigation into the issue, he generates a solution to the problem and expresses it through the character Lady Philosophy.

LADY PHILOSOPHY'S ANSWER

The common opinion, according to all people living, is that God is eternal. Let us therefore consider what eternity is. For I think the definition of eternity will clarify both the divine nature and divine foreknowledge at the same time. Eternity is the simultaneous and complete possession of infinite life. This definition will make more sense if we compare eternity with temporal existence.

All things living under the conditions of time move through the present from the past to the future. Nothing living in time can at one moment grasp the whole space of its lifetime. We cannot yet comprehend tomorrow, yesterday is already lost, and today is no more than a changing, passing moment. What we rightly call eternal, in contrast, is that which grasps and possesses wholly and simultaneously the fullness of unending life. It lacks nothing of the future, and has lost nothing of the past.

God's judgment is in a condition of ever-present eternity and all judgment apprehends the subjects of its thought according to its own nature. Therefore, God's knowledge, which encompasses every period of time, comprehends everything in its own direct view as though it were taking place in the present. So God's 'providence' is more correctly considered to be knowledge of a never-failing constancy in the present than a foreknowledge of the future. God is looking forth rather than looking forward, because he is positioned far from the temporal flow. He looks down upon our lowly temporal progress as from a lofty mountain-top above all.

If at this point you were to say that what God sees for our future cannot fail to happen, and that what cannot fail to happen is a necessity, I will admit that you're right, but only because there are two different types of necessity. Simple necessity is required by the nature of a thing. For example, it is simply necessary that all human beings are mortal. Conditional necessity, in contrast, is the result of the relation of one thing to something else. For example, if you know someone is walking, then it is necessary that he is walking. Whatever anyone truly knows cannot be otherwise than as it is known. But this doesn't imply that the walking is simply necessary. For no necessity forces someone to walk of his own will, even though it is necessary that he is walking if I see him doing it. Hence, when a future event is related to divine knowledge it is necessary but when it is considered in its own nature it is utterly and absolutely free.

In this passage, Boethius presents his famous definition of eternity as the 'simultaneous and complete possession of infinite life.' His picture of the contrast between divine eternity and human temporality is consistent with Augustine's anti-realism. Since God is the ultimate reality, and there is no passage of time for him, time is not real. Time is just a feature of the way human beings experience things.

Boethius goes beyond Augustine, however, in drawing out the logical consequences of this view. If time is not real for God, then God does not have foreknowledge. Foreknowledge is knowledge of the future. But there is no future from God's point of view. What we perceive as past, present, and future are all *now* for God. Boethius suggests an analogy to illustrate his point when he says 'God is looking forth rather than looking forward, because he is positioned far from the temporal flow. He looks down upon our lowly temporal progress as from a lofty mountain-top above all.'

Imagine you are standing by the side of the road watching a parade. As each part of the parade passes, you have to wait to find out what comes next. This is like the timeline of history as we experience it. Now imagine someone standing on a mountain that towers over the road down which the parade is proceeding. He can see the whole parade at once from this vantage point. God is like the man on the mountain above while we are like someone standing alongside the road below. We experience the timeline of history in succession; he experiences it all at once.

We can represent Boethius's argument in analogy form as follows:

1. A man on a mountain top is to the road below as God is to the timeline of history.

2. The man on the mountaintop sees the entire road in a single glance.

---

3. Therefore, God sees the entire timeline of history in a single glance.

Boethius is saying that the whole problem with divine foreknowledge arises from supposing God knows things in advance. For example, we said above that today God knows that tomorrow the king will decide to execute Boethius. This takes away the king's ability to set Boethius free. Boethius insists, however, that there is no today or tomorrow for God. God sees the king deciding to execute Boethius exactly when he decides to execute Boethius, not beforehand. This makes all of God's knowledge of our future just like our knowledge of the present. You can know for certain that someone is sitting down when she is sitting down without ever guaranteeing that she was going to sit down in the first place.

Boethius grants that certainty wouldn't be certainty unless it was necessary. But the necessity involved in certainty is different from the necessity that takes away free will. Boethius calls the necessity that takes away free will **simple necessity**, and defines it as a requirement of nature. For example, it is simply necessary that all human beings are mortal. This means we don't have a choice about dying. We all have to die. Boethius calls the necessity that does not take away free will **conditional necessity** and defines it as the result of a relationship. For example, it is conditionally necessary that if someone truly sees you walking, then you must be walking, even though nothing required you to walk in the first place.

Boethius's distinction between simple and conditional necessity is a logical distinction that can be schematized as follows:

Simple Necessity:

If X, then necessarily Y

(If you are human, then necessarily you must die.)

Conditional Necessity:

Necessarily (If X, then Y)

Necessarily (If you are seen walking, then you are walking.)

In logical terms, we can describe this distinction as follows: for simple necessity, the necessity governs the consequent of the conditional; for conditional necessity, the necessity governs the relationship between the antecedent and the consequent of the conditional.

So we can think of Boethius as rejecting premise (2) of the

sceptic's argument. Boethius would grant that, if our decisions can go either way, then God can't *know in advance* which way they will go. This would make our decisions simply necessary. But God can know which way our decisions will go from his eternal vantage point, since this makes them only conditionally necessary.

Although Boethius's logical clarity on this issue has been widely celebrated, his solution to the problem is not without its detractors. One rather bizarre implication of Boethius's view is that God does not know what day it is.

Let's say that today is 16 December 2007. Every human being around the globe knows this, or could know this by simply checking a calendar. Even though we have divided the earth into different time zones, it's not as though we are all living at different times. All humans live at the same exact time, which gives us a basis for interacting. You could call someone on the other side of the globe and speak to her in the same present moment. God, however, does not live within the temporal continuum, according to Boethius. It is not 16 December 2007 for him. It is all days at the same time for him.

In fact, there is no way for God to know what day it is for us because this would mean knowing that whatever lies beyond that day is the future for us. All the knowledge he has of that future would then be advance knowledge and we would be stuck with the original problem!

Does it matter that God does not know what day it is? Some contend that this spoils his omniscience. Others worry that it puts God in such a different reality from ours that there is no real basis for a personal relationship. Think about how many of your personal relationships depend upon remembering the past and anticipating the future. If Boethius is correct, God can't do any of this. To what extent, then, does it make sense to talk to God or even about him?

Eckhart's mysticism

Theists always run into a tension between conceiving of God as personal and conceiving of God as transcendent, meaning beyond our comprehension. In fact, God's special characteristics generate so many puzzles that God begins to seem inconceivable. Perhaps this is why Anselm defines God as 'that than which no greater can be conceived' rather than the 'greatest conceivable being.'

Realizing that the attempt to conceive of God leads to greater and greater mysteries, Meister Eckhart became convinced that it is futile to try to say anything definite about God. Joining with others who had come to this conclusion, Eckhart helped to advance the cause of negative theology.

Negative theology is the study of God through what may not be said about him. So, for example, rather than saying that God is eternal and then trying to define eternity, a negative theologian would say that God is beyond time, thereby indicating how God differs from humans without specifying the difference in a way that leads to more questions.

MEISTER ECKHART 1260–1328

Meister Eckhart was from central Germany and received his education from the Dominican Order, the 'Order of the Preachers' or 'O.P.' Despite the widespread popularity of Aristotle during this time, Eckhart became a neoplatonist, and thus a throwback to the early middle ages. His interest in supernatural phenomena eventually led him away from philosophy and towards mysticism instead.

Despite his successes first as a student and then as a teacher at the University of Paris, Eckhart soon faced criticism for his mystical ideas. A papal inquisition found him guilty of heresy. He is reported to have died just before receiving his sentence, but a record of his death and burial has never been found.

In the later middle ages positive theology began to grow like a weed in the universities. It seemed that each new solution accomplished nothing except generating a whole host of new problems to be solved. Meister Eckhart came to see this proliferation of hypotheses about God as a big mistake, as he indicates in the following passage from his *Commentary on Exodus*.

GOD IS BEYOND OUR UNDERSTANDING

The sages declare that it is dangerous, harmful, and unsuitable to hear someone piling up words about God – even in prayer – due to the imperfection which names and words entail. The qualities we observe in objects exist in a formal sense. But there are no formal qualities in God, because this would destroy God's simplicity. There are only virtual qualities in God and virtual qualities cannot be understood in the same way.

Understanding is necessarily confined to the intellect; it can never escape this limit. Therefore, the perfections of the objects we observe are not true perfections, and to attribute them to God is to apprehend him impurely. As a result, we can never truly understand God. Any such attempt is empty and erroneous.

Meister Eckhart goes on to assert that God is the 'negation of a negation.' Negative theology is a form of mysticism because it sees God as a mystery that cannot be solved.

While mystics abandon the effort to understand God, philosophers persist due to the following question. Why should you believe in something you can't comprehend? If you can't comprehend God at all, then your only basis for believing would be because someone told you to believe, and that's not a very good basis. If someone told you to believe in a completely incomprehensible monster called the Ooooshkamoosh, would you? Surely not.

Why then are so many people willing to believe in God? Because God, unlike the Ooooshkamoosh, makes some sense.

Many people believe that medieval philosophers made great progress in clarifying our understanding of God even if they did not settle everything once and for all.

As is evident from this chapter, the notion of eternity gives rise to a wealth of deep philosophical problems. Augustine and Boethius were pioneers both in identifying them and in elaborating solutions. Their solutions continue to stimulate further speculation on the nature of time and its relation to God.

5

Cosmological proof of God

Teach thy tongue to say 'I do not know,'
and thou shalt progress.

Maimonides

In ancient times people didn't know whether or not the world
was round and they didn't know whether or not it moves. In
chapter 1, we saw that Plato and Aristotle made compelling
philosophical arguments on both of these topics. Now that we
have incontrovertible evidence that the world is round and that
it moves, these topics are no longer up for philosophical debate.
Nevertheless, there are other cosmological questions that have
not yet been settled. Some of these questions are so complicated
that it seems we will never know the answer. Bear in mind,
however, that it was hard for ancient people to imagine how it
would ever be determined that the world is round and that it
moves. Throughout history, philosophers have always led the
way into the unknown.

One of the most intriguing cosmological questions we still
face concerns the age of the universe. This topic was opened for
debate in ancient times and, though few people realize, it is still
rigorously debated today. Medieval philosophers defined two
opposing positions that capture the issue.

Modern views of the universe

Today everyone learns in school that the universe as we know it started with a cosmic explosion called the 'big bang.' We know about this explosion because we observe that the universe is expanding. By tracing the pattern of expansion backwards, astrophysicists have determined that, around fourteen billion years ago, the universe was compressed into an extremely hot, dense state that burst apart, pushing outer space and all of its contents in every direction.

The big bang is such an excellent theory that it is widely accepted as fact. Many people are content to conclude therefore that the universe is fourteen billion years old and call the issue settled. But the big bang really only serves to highlight a bigger question that still needs to be answered, namely, what happened before the big bang?

For some people, the big bang was the absolute beginning, meaning that there was nothing at all happening before it. This view is a perfect match for the story of creation told in the major monotheistic religions. Proponents of this view may disagree over exactly how long ago the universe began, but they agree that God created the universe *ex nihilo*, or out of nothing, some finite number of years ago. This is the **creation model** of the universe.

There is no evidence, however, that the big bang was the absolute beginning, and there is some indication that it wasn't. Many astrophysicists believe that our universe cannot go on expanding forever. At some point it will run out of momentum and gravity will pull everything back together again into a 'big crunch.' The big crunch will result in a state so hot and dense that it will have to explode into another big bang, thereby producing another expanding universe. If this is the case, then it seems likely that the big bang that resulted in the universe we know today is itself the result of the big crunch of a prior universe. The same would be said for that prior universe, and so on, ad infinitum. This succession of universes is actually just the same universe oscillating through expansion and contraction through all of eternity. Proponents of this view maintain that there is no absolute beginning; the universe has always existed. This is called the **oscillating model** of the universe.

When people first hear of the oscillating model they often say: 'Well, it could be that the universe has undergone a number of oscillations in this manner, but there has to have been a first one at some point, and this is the moment of creation.'

According to the oscillating model, however, there does not have to be a moment of creation. On the contrary, the universe does not need to be created on this model because it has existed for all eternity. Although this claim about eternity is unfamiliar, it isn't any more far fetched, *ex hypothesi*, than the creation model. According to the creation model, God has existed for all eternity. If it is possible to conceive of a God who has always existed and never had a beginning, then it is equally possible to conceive of a universe that has always existed and never had a beginning.

Since the oscillating model has no moment of creation, it is not a perfect match for the creation stories of the major monotheistic religions. In fact, for some people, it shows there is no need to believe in God at all. Once you believe in an eternal world there is no role for a creator to play. Others, however, see the oscillating universe as coexisting for all eternity with God, as a divine emanation rather than as a creation. This interpretation borders on pantheism, the view that everything is God, because an emanation flows from its source as a continuous part of it.

Needless to say, medieval philosophers did not know about the big bang or the big crunch. Nevertheless, they clearly identified the same two positions: created world versus eternal world. Plato argued for the former and Aristotle argued for the latter, thereby leaving medieval philosophers to take sides.

Aquinas's first way

Thomas Aquinas defends the creation model. Though agreeing with Plato's conclusion, he departs from Plato in using empirical observations to make his case. The claim that the universe must have had a beginning forms the basis of an argument that has come to be known the '**cosmological proof** of the existence of God.' Aquinas famously presents five empiricist proofs of the existence of God. The cosmological, also known as the argument from motion, is the first of the five. You will find it in the passage below, which is taken from a work called the *Summa Theologica*.

THERE MUST HAVE BEEN A BEGINNING

The first and most compelling way to prove the existence of God is the argument from motion. It is evident to the senses that some things in the world are in motion. Moreover, whatever is in motion is put in motion by something else.

Nothing can be in motion unless it was once in a state of potentiality for that motion. Motion is nothing other than something changing from a state of potentiality to a state of actuality. So a thing moves inasmuch as it is in action. But nothing can be changed from potentiality to actuality except by something that is already in a state of actuality. This is true not just of motion but of any kind of change. For example, fire is actually hot while wood is potentially hot. Fire makes wood actually hot and thereby changes it.

It is not possible for something to be in a state of actuality and potentiality at the same time and in the same respect. For example, wood can be both potentially hot and actually hot, but not at the same time and in the same respect. Rather, wood that is actually hot is simultaneously potentially cold. It has to change from one state to the other.

This point about change applies directly to motion. It is impossible for a thing to be both a mover and a thing moved at the same time and in the same respect because then it would have to move itself.

If something in motion must be put in motion by another thing, then that other thing must also be put in motion by another, and that by another, and so on, and so on. But this cannot go on to infinity. There has to be a first mover. If there were no first mover, then there would be no second mover and no subsequent movers at all. Subsequent movers move only because they are put in motion by the first mover.

Suppose I have a stick in my hand and I'm using it to push a stone. The stone moves because of the stick, but the stick moves only because it is put in motion by my hand. The same holds true for the motion of the things in the world. Tracing backward, it is necessary to arrive at a first mover. The first mover would move things without itself being moved. This unmoved mover is what everyone means by 'God.'

Elsewhere in his writings, Aquinas credits Aristotle's arguments for an eternal world. This passage, however, is typically interpreted as an empiricist defence of the creation model: the motion we observe had to have a beginning and this beginning must have been God.

Aquinas launches his argument with the explicitly empiricist observation that things in the world are in motion. He then goes on to examine the nature of motion. If we limit ourselves to inanimate objects, it is evident that things don't move all by themselves. For example, the sand is moved by the waves, the waves are moved by the wind, and so on. In each case we can point to a prior cause of the motion. Although animate objects, such as plants, animals, and human beings, appear to move themselves, upon closer examination it is evident that their motions have prior causes as well. The sun causes the sunflower to lean to the east; a hawk causes a mouse to scurry into a hole; a ring tone causes Joe to reach for his phone. In each case we see a sequence of cause and effect.

Aquinas goes on to define motion as a change from potentiality to actuality. A rock sitting at the top of the hill has the potential to roll down the hill. If Joe pushes the rock, then he is the mover and the rock is the thing moved. As mover, Joe is in actuality. As he pushes the rock it changes from potentiality to actuality. Potentiality and actuality are opposite states. Because of this, nothing can have both at the same time in the same respect. If the rock knocks over a flower as it reaches the bottom of the hill, then it is both a mover and a thing moved. But it is a mover with respect to the flower and a thing moved with respect to Joe. So it is not both a mover and a thing moved at the same time and in the same respect. In order for the rock to be both a mover and a thing moved at the same time and in the same respect it would have to push itself down the hill. This is impossible, because it cannot go from the state of potentiality to the opposite state of actuality without some kind of cause.

Having established that all motion requires a sequence of cause and effect, Aquinas applies this pattern to the entire history of the world. His argument can be reconstructed in valid form as follows:

1. Something is in motion.

2. If something is in motion, then it must be put in motion by something else.

3. If something in motion must be put in motion by something else, then either things put things in motion ad infinitum or there is an unmoved mover that can put things in motion without itself being moved.

4. It is impossible for things to put things in motion ad infinitum.

5. So, there is an unmoved mover that can put things in motion without itself being moved.

6. The unmoved mover that can put things in motion without itself being moved is God.

---

7. Therefore, there is a God.

By casting God as the unmoved mover, Aquinas conceives of God as pure actuality. Because God has within him no potentiality, he cannot be moved by anything else.

Although there are a number of controversial steps in the argument, critics have often focused on premise (4). Why does Aquinas think it is impossible for things to put things in motion ad infinitum? Those who agree with Aquinas on this point tend to argue as follows. If there were no first motion, then we would have to traverse an infinity of motions in order to arrive at the present motion. But it is impossible to traverse an infinity. Therefore there must be a first motion. This argument insists that an infinite sequence of cause and effect is impossible.

It might be objected, however, that whether or not an infinite sequence of cause and effect is impossible depends on how you conceive of infinity. Consider, for example, an ancient puzzle known as **Zeno's paradox**. Suppose you want to traverse a road from point A to point B. In order to do this, you have to go half way first. Call the halfway mark between point A and point B 'point C.' In order to travel to point C, you will have to go half way first. Call the halfway mark between point A and point C 'point D.' To travel to point D, you will once again have to go half way first. The same reasoning applies again and again without end because there is a halfway mark between every two points, no matter how close they are. You would never be able to traverse the road because it would require an infinite number of journeys. This result is a paradox, because we all know perfectly well that, in reality, you can traverse the road.

Zeno's paradox arises from thinking of the halfway marks on the road as an actual infinite. An **actual infinite** is a set with infinitely many members. It is impossible to traverse an actual infinite because the distance is infinitely long. Just as we could never traverse Zeno's road if that road is a set of infinitely many halfway marks, we could never arrive at the present moment if the past is a set of infinitely many moments.

There are all sorts of problems with the very notion of an actual infinity. Imagine an infinitely long road with cars parked at the curb end-to-end along the entire road. Clearly, there must be an infinite number of cars. Suppose each car is either white or black and that they are parked in alternate colours. There must be an infinite number of white cars as well as an infinite number of black cars. But how can there be just as many white cars as there are white and black cars put together? Further, suppose every car has a driver sitting at the wheel. But now one more person arrives who would like a car to drive. So we ask all the drivers to get out of their cars and move one car back. This frees a car for the extra driver. So does this mean we have more than an infinite set now? No, because it is impossible to exceed infinity. Does it mean we have infinity now but had less than infinity before? No, because we could do the same thing again. After considering thought experiments along these lines many people conclude that an actual infinite is an incoherent concept.

A **potential infinite**, in contrast, is an unending sequence of numbers to count. Since numbers are not actually existing things like cars, the problems discussed in the last paragraph cannot arise. Moreover, if we think of Zeno's road in terms of a potential infinite, then it is not infinitely long. On this view, the 'halfway marks' are just mental markers. Although there is no end to the numbers we can count, those numbers don't exist on the road. So, while it is impossible ever to finish counting halfway marks, it is not impossible to traverse the road.

To say that the past is a potential infinite is to say that, if we started counting moments backward, we would never arrive at a first moment. Instead, we would have to keep counting backwards forever, as we would with the 'negative' numbers that come before zero (–1, –2, –3, –4, –5 . . .). On this view, measuring the past is like enumerating an unending sequence of numbers. Since they exist only in the mind and not in the world, they do not create an infinite distance to traverse. Notice that this view amounts to temporal anti-realism, which we examined in the last chapter, because it casts time as a mental measurement.

It is evident that Aquinas is committed to temporal realism, according to which time exists independently of the mind. When he thinks of the past as a sequence of moments, he thinks of these moments as lining up to form a distance that has to be traversed. This is why the past cannot be infinite in his view. Temporal anti-realists, however, deny that the past exists independently of the mind. By conceiving of moments as mental markers they have a way to refute premise (4) of Aquinas's argument: it is possible for things to put things in motion ad infinitum because an unending number of moments to count does not result in an infinite distance that has to be traversed.

While temporal anti-realism provides one possible line of defence against the cosmological argument, another famous line of defence comes from within the temporal realist camp.

Averroes's eternal world

Although Aquinas popularized the cosmological argument in Europe, he did not invent it. The idea was originally laid out by Plato and then developed to a very sophisticated degree by Islamic philosophers in the Middle East.

After the fall of the Roman Empire, Europe declined into the 'dark ages.' From around 550 to around 1050 every day was a struggle and there was little time for cultural pursuits such as philosophy. The opposite was true, however, in the Middle

East. Mohamed, the founder of the Muslim religion, ignited a revolution around the turn of the seventh century that led to a golden age for the Islamic Empire. While Christians languished, Muslims thrived, extending their territory from Spain to Madagascar to India. During this period Muslims made many advances in technology and other cultural pursuits, including philosophy.

Intellectuals throughout the European middle ages always had to develop their ideas within confines set by the Catholic Church. Likewise, Muslim intellectuals were constantly balancing philosophy with religion. They discovered the works of Plato and Aristotle and translated them into Arabic, always careful to interpret them in a manner consistent with the Koran. Two strong factions emerged among Muslim intellectuals. Those who adhered conservatively to the traditional religious teachings were known as the 'theologians.' Those who liberally reinterpreted the traditional religious teachings to fit with scientific and philosophical theory were known as the 'philosophers.'

The theologians developed a practice, called 'kalam,' of seeking theological truth through dialectic. One of the most famous results of this practice is known as 'The Kalam Cosmological Argument.' It is the obvious source for Aquinas's 'First Way.' Although there are a number of different versions, they all assert that the universe began to exist at a definite point in the past and, because of this, it must have a cause. Just like Aquinas, the Muslim theologians insist that the universe could not have eternally coexisted with God. They believe that the Koran, like the Bible, clearly states that God created the world.

Averroes was a Muslim philosopher who resisted the theologians' traditional interpretation of the Koran. He maintains instead that the universe has always existed as an eternal emanation from God. The leading theologian Al Ghazali wrote a work called *The Incoherence of the Philosophers* attacking this and other liberal departures from the Koran. Averroes responded

---

AVERROES 1126–1198

Averroes was an Arabic philosopher born in Cordoba, Spain, which was then part of the Muslim empire. Although he wrote in Arabic, his works were quickly translated into Latin and spread to the Christian regions of Europe. The name 'Averroes' is actually a Latinization of his true name, Ibn Rushd.

Although trained in medicine as well as jurisprudence, Averroes's first love was philosophy. An avid Aristotelian, he helped to revive interest in Aristotle. Because Averroes wrote extensive and highly respected commentaries on Aristotle's works, he became known as 'The Commentator.'

Averroes worked as physician and judge for the Almohad prince of his region, who was very liberal and supportive of philosophy. Public opinion eventually turned against these liberal tendencies, however. Eventually, Averroes was exiled and his works were burned. Although his reputation was somewhat restored before he died, he was widely regarded with suspicion from then on within both the Muslim and the Christian worlds.

---

quid pro quo with a work called *The Incoherence of 'The Incoherence.'* His main argument for eternal emanation is found in the passage below from this work.

THERE WAS NO BEGINNING

The greatest challenge the theologians raise for the philosophers is this: If the movements in the past are infinite, then no movement in the actual present can take place. To arrive at the present, it would be necessary to complete an infinite number of movements, which is impossible.

We, the philosophers, reply as follows. If we were to grant that the prior movement is a necessary condition for the posterior movement's taking place, then their argument would be sound. That is, if we were to allow that there is a movement which causes an infinite number of movements, then our cause would be lost. But we do not allow this. It is the materialists who allow for the existence of an infinite number of causes. Their view is flawed because it implies the existence of an effect without cause and a motion without mover.

According to our view, in contrast, there is an eternal prime mover whose act is eternally simultaneous with his being. It follows that there cannot be a beginning for his act any more than there can be a beginning for his being. If there were a beginning for his act, then this act would not be necessary, and he would not be the first principle.

The acts of an agent who has no beginning have a beginning as little as his existence, and therefore it follows necessarily that no preceding act of his is the condition for the existence of a later, for neither of them is an agent by itself and their sequence is accidental.

An accidental infinite, not an essential infinite, is admitted by the philosophers. This type of infinite is in fact a necessary consequence of the existence of an eternal first principle. This is not only true for successive or continuous movements like the planetary motions, but even where the earlier is regarded as the cause of the later, for instance the human being who engenders another human being. For it is necessary that the series of temporal productions of one individual by another, while itself horizontal, should be related vertically to an eternal agent, for whom there is no beginning either of his existence or of his production of human from human. The production of one human by another ad infinitum is accidental, whereas the relation of before and after within the production is essential.

In this passage Averroes argues that since the universe is produced by God, it must be co-eternal with him. He pictures the universe as a divine emanation rather than as a divine creation. Although this stretches the meaning of the Koran, it does provide a handy solution to the problem of divine idleness that we looked at in the last chapter: there was never a time before God created the world because God and the world have always coexisted.

Averroes's position is built on a distinction between two different types of sequence: accidentally ordered and essentially ordered.

In an **essentially ordered sequence**, posterior members of the sequence depend on prior members of the sequence for their existence. Suppose, for example, you see four cars parked end-to-end at the corner of the street. You soon discover that this configuration is the result of multi-car pile-up. The first car stopped suddenly, causing the second car to crash into it. The sudden stopping of the second car caused the third car to crash into the second car. The sudden stopping of the third car likewise caused the fourth car to crash. So, the first car caused the second car's crash, which caused the third car's crash, which caused the fourth car's crash. This is an essentially ordered sequence because each crash depends for its existence on the prior car stopping suddenly.

We can use the following diagram to illustrate an essentially ordered sequence:

In this diagram, 'A' is the first car, which is the 'first cause' of the pile-up. The causal relationship is horizontal.

In an **accidentally ordered sequence**, in contrast, posterior members of the sequence do not depend on prior members of the sequence for their existence. Suppose, for example, you again see three cars parked end-to-end at the corner of the street. This time, however, you learn that the drivers stopped their cars there because it was free parking for the corner market.

Each car stopped in relation to the market not in relation to the car ahead.

We can use the following diagram to illustrate an accidentally ordered sequence:

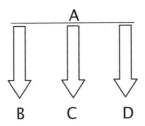

In this diagram, 'A' is the market, which is the 'first cause' of the parking configuration. The causal relationship is vertical.

Averroes is a temporal realist like Aquinas. Moreover, he agrees with Aquinas's claim that it is impossible for things to put things in motion ad infinitum. But he disagrees with Aquinas's reason for this claim. For Aquinas, if things put things in motion ad infinitum, the result would be an actually infinite set of moments, which could never be traversed in order to arrive at the present. Averroes, on the other hand, insists that an actually infinite set of moments is only a problem if it is conceived as an essentially ordered sequence. If one moment has to cause the next moment, which has to cause the next moment, then we would never arrive at the present. An actually infinite set of moments is not a problem, however, if it is conceived as an accidentally ordered sequence. Each moment in the timeline of history is caused directly by God rather than being caused by the prior moment. On this view there is no beginning to the timeline any more than there is a beginning to God.

Averroes's argument can be represented in valid form as follows.

1. God is eternal.
2. If God is eternal, then his every act must be eternal.

3. One of God's acts is his production of the world.

4. So, God's production of the world must be eternal.

5. If God's production of the world is eternal, then prior moments don't cause posterior moments.

6. If prior moments don't cause posterior moments, then every moment has always existed.

7. If every moment has always existed, then there can be no beginning to the past.

---

8. Therefore, there can be no beginning to the past.

Based on this argument, Averroes insists that the Koran should be interpreted in terms of divine emanation rather than creation.

The most controversial aspect of Averroes's proposal is his suggestion, crucially supporting premise (5), that the timeline of history is an accidentally ordered series. This goes against the way we think about time. As Averroes himself admits, when we observe successive events we regard the earlier as the cause of the later. For instance, when Sarah has a baby, it seems obvious that the pregnancy causes the birth. On Averroes's view, however, God caused the birth directly. He also caused the pregnancy. But no preceding act of God is the condition for the existence of a later act of God. So, from God's point of view, the pregnancy and the birth are eternally simultaneous and the connection between the two events is 'accidental,' by which Averroes means unnecessary.

The idea that there is no necessity in the (horizontal) connection between cause and effect because God causes each event vertically is called **occasionalism.** Although occasionalism was embraced by some of Averroes's fellow Arabic philosophers, Averroes himself tried to maintain that his view does not imply occasionalism. The reason is that occasionalism has some rather off-putting implications.

For example, responsibility seems to require a necessary connection between cause and effect. We might say that when the pyromaniac set the house on fire he caused the death of a sleeping infant. According to the occasionalist, however, the connection between the pyromaniac's action and the death of the infant is only accidental. God is directly responsible for both. If this is the case then how can we hold the pyromaniac accountable – for either reformative or retributive justice? Some would say that removing the necessary connection between cause and effect also destroys the foundation of science. For example, the occcasionalist can't say that smoking causes lung cancer but only that lung cancer is usually preceded by smoking.

Notice that, at the end of the passage on page 103, Averroes writes 'The production of one human being by another ad infinitum is accidental, whereas the relation of before and after within the production is essential.' This seems to be how he hopes to escape occasionalism. Since there is no before-and-after from God's point of view, there is no necessary connection between cause and effect from God's point of view. Since there is before-and-after from the human point of view, however, there is a necessary connection between cause and effect from the human point of view.

But how convincing is this compromise? It seems that either eternal emanation is sufficient to account for the production of the world or it isn't. If it is sufficient, then horizontal causality is ultimately an illusion, just as the occasionalist insists. If it isn't sufficient, then we need something else to account for horizontal causality. Whatever this is would surely either have a beginning or generate the very same infinite regress that Averroes has been trying to avoid.

Maimonides's agnosticism

While not many medievals jumped on Averroes's bandwagon in favour of the eternal emanation model, his argument nevertheless served to undermine confidence in the temporal creation model. That is, many subsequent philosophers affirmed the creation model, while at the same time admitting that it cannot be decisively proven. This situation has persisted to the present day: while most astrophysicists favour the big bang model, they recognize that the oscillating model cannot be discounted.

In his most famous work, *The Guide for the Perplexed*, Maimonides presents a provocative analogy designed to show that the issue cannot be settled by argument. You will find it in the passage below.

IT CAN'T BE DETERMINED

It is a mistake to attempt to prove the nature of a thing in potential existence by its properties when actually existing. If you do this you will fall into great confusion, rejecting evident truths and accepting false opinions.

Suppose a woman gives birth to a healthy baby boy but she dies after nursing him for only a few months. The father raises the boy on a lonely island where there are no other females. The boy grows to be a wise man, who nevertheless has no idea how human beings come into existence. He asks someone and is told that human beings begin their existence as very small living beings in the womb of a woman, where they move, receive nourishment, and grow, until they finally come out. The man will naturally ask whether these small beings breathe with their mouths and their nostrils while in the womb. The answer will be no. So then the man will undoubtedly attempt to refute the explanation and prove its impossibility by referring to the properties of a fully developed human being. He might say 'When any one of us is deprived of breath for a short time we die and cannot move any longer. How then can we imagine that any one of us has been enclosed in a bag in someone's body for several months while remaining alive and able to move? If any one of us would swallow a living bird, it would probably die immediately when it reached the stomach, or at least when it came to the lower part of the belly.' This mode of reasoning would lead to the conclusion that human beings cannot come into existence and develop in the manner described.

If philosophers would consider this example well and reflect on it, they would find that it represents exactly the dispute at hand.

Maimonides's point is that there is no reason to think that rules that apply to the universe as we see it now apply to considerations about its distant history.

Maimonides's analogy can be reconstructed as follows:

1. Conception is to a human being as creation is to the universe.

2. Rules that apply to human beings now may not apply at conception.

---

3. Therefore, rules that apply to the universe now may not apply at creation.

This leaves Maimonides in an agnostic state of mind on the issue: we really can't know for sure whether the creation or the emanation model is true.

Maimonides sees Muslim philosophers like Averroes making the same mistake as the man in his analogy. Looking around the world today, we can affirm that the principle *nihil ex nihilo* holds true: nothing comes from nothing. That is to say, no material thing simply pops into existence. Trees come from seeds and soil; rivers come from springs; statues come from clay; etc. The creation model contradicts this principle by claiming that God created the world *ex nihilo*. Maimonides thinks Averroes advances his eternal emanation theory in order to avoid contradicting this principle. Against this strategy, Maimonides insists that even if it is true now that nothing comes from nothing, it may not have been true at the moment of creation.

MAIMONIDES c. 1138–1204

Moses ben Maimon, also known as Maimonides, was a Jewish philosopher born in Cordoba, Spain, less than a generation after Averroes. Although Cordoba was a major cultural center, the Arab rule of this area was growing increasingly intolerant of Jews. When Maimonides was ten years old the Almohad prince issued all Jews a choice of conversion, exile, or death. Maimonides's family chose exile. After wandering *passim* through southern Spain for a number of years they settled in Morocco. Here Maimonides wrote his first of a series of theological works that would earn him the title 'greatest Jewish philosopher of the middle ages.'

Maimonides moved to Cairo, Egypt when he was twenty-eight and began work on his masterpiece, *The Guide for the Perplexed*. It is framed as a letter to a student who cannot decide whether to pursue theology or philosophy. Although it covers many topics, its underlying theme is the relation between faith and reason. The *Guide* has always been considered controversial and was originally banned in some Jewish circles. Christian philosophers throughout Europe read Maimonides avidly but rarely credited him for fear of being associated with Judaism.

Maimonides's point also cuts against Christian philosophers like Aquinas who argue that, by observing cause and effect among things that move, we can infer that the universe is the effect of a first cause. Everything we see around us in the world has a beginning. It is tempting to assume therefore that the universe as a whole must have a beginning too. But there is no contradiction in supposing that the universe is infinitely old. Hence, the eternal emanation model could be correct.

As a committed Jew, Maimonides accepts the creation model in the end, but only on faith. The question, in his view, cannot be determined by rational argument. Returning to his analogy, he would recommend that the man who had never seen a pregnant woman should accept the testimony of a trustworthy witness. For Maimonides, the prophets of the Old Testament are trustworthy witnesses whose testimony should be accepted.

It is interesting to note that even when Averroes rejected the creation model, he never questioned the existence of God. On the contrary, for him, the eternity model relies just as heavily on a prime mover as does the creation model. Nevertheless, it is easy to see why many theists, whether Christian, Muslim, or Jewish, were threatened by the eternity model. Casting the universe as a brute fact that has always been and always will be leaves little role for God to play.

Medieval philosophers are famous for raising the question: Why is there something rather than nothing? They believed there is a reason for the universe, a reason that leads directly to God. Few of them were willing to entertain the hypothesis that there may be no reason at all.

6

Teleological proof of God

It is futile to do with more what can be done with less.
William of Ockham

In the last chapter we saw that it is not so easy to prove the existence of God on the grounds that there had to be someone to start the universe up. Since it could be that the universe has always been going in some form or other, theists have to look elsewhere for evidence of God. Upon realizing this, some turn from the sheer existence of the universe to its organization, seeking proof of God in the fact that the universe contains conditions perfect for advanced life forms.

When we look around the natural world we observe an extraordinary degree of complexity at all levels. For example, the ecosystem in a rainforest is a delicate balance of competitive and cooperative relationships. Mammals feed on plants which, in turn, feed on the soil. If any of the links in the chain breaks, catastrophe could strike the entire system. Yet the system is resilient. Life finds a way. Consider also the intricate workings of minute parts of the system, such as the eyeball of a monkey. With all of our technological advancements, human beings still have not even come close to replicating an instrument of such power and precision. Yet nature produces eyeballs of many different kinds as a matter of course over and over again. Nature is a spectacularly beautiful and awe-inspiring phenomenon.

Thinking along these lines through the ages, human beings have often arrived the following thought: Surely the natural world could not have come about by accident. It must have been designed by a supreme being. This thought is the intuition behind the **teleological proof** of the existence of God. The name comes from the Greek word 'telos,' which means design or purpose.

Ancient views of nature

Formal debate over the design of the natural world began in ancient Greece with a philosopher named Empedocles (490–430 BC), who elaborates an account of the history of the world that is both poetic and scientifically insightful. Empedocles holds that Love and Strife are the two controlling forces in nature. Love is responsible for bringing the basic elements of material reality together and Strife is responsible for pulling them apart. Love and Strife alternate ascendancy: as Love brings the elements together, new creatures are generated; as Strife pulls the elements apart, the creatures are destroyed. Many different creatures have evolved through this cosmic cycle. Unfortunately, we do not know much more about Empedocles's work because only fragments survive.

Aristotle read Empedocles and disagreed with him. He reports the most compelling aspect of Empedocles's theory as a challenge to his own view.

EMPEDOCLES'S EXPLANATION

Some might say nature works, not for the sake of something, nor because it is better so, but of necessity. For example, the sky rains, not in order to make the corn grow, but only because what is drawn up must cool, and what has been cooled must become water and descend. The result of this is that the corn grows. Why then should it not be the same with other aspects of nature?

For example, perhaps our teeth grow as they do of necessity. Because the front teeth are sharp they are good for shredding and because the molars are broad they are good for grinding. But perhaps the teeth did not grow this way for the purpose of chewing food. Rather, it was merely a coincident result.

The same could be said of all other parts in which we suppose that there is purpose. Wherever the parts of an animal accidentally came to exist in a fitting way, they resulted in the survival of the animal, whereas those which grew otherwise perished and continue to perish. Empedocles says this is what happened to a certain race of oxen that had human faces.

Although Empedocles's example of human-faced oxen is quite fanciful, the principle behind it, that some combinations work better than others, is not. The unfit creatures die out, leaving the accidental successes to survive. This trial and error system could easily create the illusion that someone deliberately designed the survivors.

Aristotle is not at all impressed with this idea, however. His complaint is that mere coincidence cannot explain the patterns we observe in nature. He points out that teeth and all other natural things regularly come about in the same way. But the results of chance are always different. So chance cannot be responsible for the natural world.

Aristotle's argument forms a template for Thomas Aquinas's fifth empiricist proof of the existence of God. In the previous chapter we looked at his 'first way.' The first way and the fifth way are the best of the five.

AQUINAS'S FIFTH WAY

The fifth way comes from the governance of the world. We see that things which lack intelligence, such as natural bodies, act for an end. This is evident because they always, or nearly always, act in the same way, in order to obtain the best result.

So it is clear that they achieve their end by design not by chance.

Whatever lacks intelligence cannot move towards an end unless it is directed by some being endowed with knowledge and intelligence. For example, an archer directs his arrow to an end when he shoots his target. Therefore, some intelligent being exists who directs all natural things to their end. This is what we mean by 'God.'

By 'acting for an end' Aquinas means acting purposefully. Aquinas's point is that we would not observe purpose in nature unless it was designed by someone with intelligence.

We can reconstruct Aquinas's argument in valid form as follows:

1. Unintelligent things in the world act with purpose.

2. If unintelligent things in the world act with purpose, then there must be someone with intelligence guiding them.

---

3. So, there must be someone with intelligence guiding them.

4. The only being with enough intelligence to guide them is God.

---

5. Therefore, there must be a God.

This reconstruction reveals two main vulnerable points in the argument. Someone might attack premise (4) on the grounds that earth might be the science project of some alien from outer space. That is, even if someone with intelligence designed life on earth, how do we know that it is the God worshiped in Christianity, Judaism, or Islam?

There is an even more significant problem with premise (1), however. Aquinas frames his argument as an empiricist proof on the grounds that we can observe purpose in nature. Upon closer examination this is a problematic claim. We don't actually observe purpose, but only things engaged in complex activities.

THOMAS AQUINAS 1225-1274

Thomas Aquinas was born into a noble family in a castle south of Rome in Italy. While studying at the University of Naples, he encountered the Dominican Order and decided to join.

When Aquinas announced this intention to his family, however, they captured him and confined him in a fortress for two years while they tried to convince him to change his mind. Their efforts, however, were futile. He took his vows immediately upon his release.

While in captivity, Aquinas was allowed to read the Bible and Aristotle's metaphysics, which had recently been rediscovered. His subsequent career as a philosopher is often characterized as an attempt to reconcile the two.

Before completing his degree in theology, Aquinas went to Cologne, Germany, to study with Albert the Great, an expert on the recently rediscovered Aristotle. At the University of Cologne, Aquinas acquired the unofficial nickname 'the Dumb Ox,' because he was a very large man and kept quiet because he knew no German. After completing his degree, he taught at Paris and wrote prolifically, revealing himself to be one of the greatest minds of his day.

Although his own work was sometimes regarded with suspicion, the Catholic Church trusted him to investigate a number of controversies concerning heresy. He was canonized as a saint by the Catholic Church shortly after his death.

For example, suppose you wake up one Christmas morning to discover a nativity scene etched in the frost on your bedroom window. When you go out to investigate, you see no footsteps in the snow and so you begin to think the picture is a sign from God. The morning of the next snowfall, however, you wake to find a new picture etched in the frost. This time it is an Elvis luau scene. When you go out to investigate, you realize that the branch of a nearby tree has been brushing against the window.

Sure enough, you get a new picture with each new snowfall. A tree branch brushing against a window is a physical event that can be observed while purpose is an abstract idea that cannot be observed. How do we know we aren't projecting design on to the world?

The problem with purpose

William of Ockham was the first philosopher to raise these problems concerning the teleological proof and to resurrect Empedocles's alternative. Both Aquinas and Ockham considered themselves devoted followers of Aristotle, whom they called the 'Philosopher' in accordance with medieval custom. Nevertheless, Ockham was even more devoted to empiricism than he was to Aristotle. Hence Ockham boldly reinterprets Aristotle or even takes issue with him whenever Aristotle wanders from the path of pure observation. In so doing he often ran the risk of upsetting the university authorities on two counts: first, for taking liberties with a highly esteemed text; and second, for pushing empiricism to the point where it threatens religious belief.

Ockham typically tries to soften his rebellious departures. In the following passage, however, his deference to authority does not prevent him from completely undermining the teleological proof.

PURPOSE IS NOT OBSERVABLE

If I accepted no authority, I would claim that it cannot be proven, either from statements known in themselves or from experience, that every effect is directed toward an end.

Someone who is just following natural reason would claim that the question 'Why?' is inappropriate in the case of natural actions. He would maintain that questions like, 'Why is there fire?' have no real answer at all.

Just as the rain falls on the corn fields of necessity, nothing prevents the parts of animals from coming about due to the necessity of nature. The necessity of nature brings it about that the parts in some animals are conveniently arranged for the health of the whole.

For example, the front teeth are sharp and apt for shredding food while the molars are flat and apt for grinding food. The front teeth would become sharp and the back would become flat, however, even if they were not apt for these uses. Thus they did not come into being because of such uses. Just as it is with these parts of animals, so also it is with the other parts of the animals that would come to be just as they are from the necessity of matter, although no uses were intended. Consequently these parts do not exist because of such uses. Rather, when they come to be, then the animals survive.

The reason is this: A certain disposition of parts promotes the health of the animal. But these parts become apt for conserving the animal by chance. In fact, they would come to be just as they are from the necessity of nature even if such a disposition were not conducive to the health of the animal.

It should be noted that the reasons Aristotle adduces against this view are not demonstrative. They will only convince an adversary who has argued poorly. For the Philosopher presupposes exactly what he is trying to prove, namely, that those things which do not happen by chance happen for a reason and that things which happen always or for the most part do not happen by chance.

The Commentator expressly states that this conclusion, namely, that every natural agent acts for a reason, cannot be demonstrated. He writes, 'Aristotle's argument can be used only against an adversary who denies the principle of nature.' From this it is evident that the conclusion is not demonstrative. Accordingly, others who want to prove this conclusion either beg the question in the same way or accept an undemonstrated conclusion. I could show this by running through their arguments, but for the sake of brevity, I pass on.

Notice that Ockham refers to Aristotle as the 'Philosopher' and to Averroes as the 'Commentator' in this passage.

Ockham's main problem with Aristotle and Aquinas is that their teleology is based on the fallacy of false dilemma. They reason as follows: the natural world must be explained either by chance or by purpose, but the patterns we observe in the natural world are far too regular to be the result of chance, so they must be the result of purpose. The choice offered in this argument completely ignores a third possibility, namely, necessity. On Ockham's account, it is actually a combination of necessity and chance that explains the patterns we observe in the natural world.

For example, it is by necessity that teeth grew in different configurations in different animals. It is by chance that one of these configurations (sharp in front, flat at the back) was especially efficient for chewing food. Those with that configuration lived on and multiplied; those with other configurations died out.

Ockham is careful to inform the reader that, in drawing these conclusions he is speaking as a scientist. As a Christian, he will be content to affirm whatever doctrines are required by the Church, but he refuses to pretend that these doctrines can be proven. As a matter of fact, Ockham rejects all of the proofs of the existence of God. We have seen that Augustine, Anselm, and Aquinas all believed that faith could be confirmed by reason and evidence. They are therefore considered **evidentialists**, Augustine and Anselm being innatist evidentialists, Aquinas being an empiricist evidentialist. Ockham, in contrast to all three, joins Maimonides in subscribing to **fideism**: the truths of religion must be taken on faith alone.

WILLIAM OF OCKHAM (OCCAM) *c.* 1285–1347

Nothing is known of William of Ockham's origin except that he was probably English. He joined the Franciscan Order at a young age and eventually commenced a degree in theology at the University of Oxford. Before he could finish it, however, he was summoned to the papal court to answer to charges of heresy.

During this period, the papal court was not in Rome but in Avignon, in the south of France. Pope John XXII was in the process of building himself an enormous palace there, complete with the largest library in all of Europe. Ockham stayed at this palace under house arrest for four years while his accusers tried to make their case against him. This proved difficult to do since Ockham was so adept at arguing!

In the meanwhile, Ockham met some other Franciscans awaiting trial. After reading the charges against them, Ockham became convinced that the pope was persecuting Franciscans because their rigorous commitment to the vow of poverty was making it difficult for the pope to justify his lavish wealth.

Ockham and his fellow Franciscans finally decided to escape. They stole some horses in the night and rode to the protection of Prince Ludwig of Bavaria. All four were promptly excommunicated and chased across Europe. Ockham lived the rest of his life in exile writing political treatises against the papacy.

Ockham's razor

Ockham's contention is that, since purpose cannot be observed, there is no justification for positing it. In his view, empiricism requires positing nothing more than you absolutely have to in order to explain what you see. Of course, natural necessity is no more observable than purpose. Ockham takes the position, however, that the regularity of the patterns we observe in nature require positing natural necessity whether you add purpose as well or not. It is better to posit natural necessity alone than to posit both natural necessity and purpose.

In taking this position, Ockham employs the **principle of simplicity**, according to which the simpler theory is more likely to be true. Ockham uses this principle so often and so effectively in his work that it came to be known as Ockham's razor. It is the *sine qua non* of his entire philosophy. The principle first appears in Aristotle, and has been closely associated with empiricism throughout the history of philosophy. Ockham typically expresses the principle by saying that it is futile to do with more what can be done with less. Another formulation is that entities should not be multiplied without necessity. All of these formulations support the empiricists' agenda because direct experience is in their view the only thing that necessitates the multiplication of entities.

Clearly, the principle of simplicity came to be known as a 'razor' because a razor is a precision instrument that scrapes away unwanted excess. It is interesting to note, however, that the razor has further significance within the medieval context. Medieval philosophers wrote all of their books by hand on parchment, which is treated animal skin. They used a quill for applying ink and a razor for erasing errors. This is useful to remember when interpreting the meaning of the principle of simplicity. The principle does not claim that the world is simple. Rather, it claims that the theories we write about the world should be as simple as possible. Every new entity or hypothesis you add comes with the danger of error. Therefore, the more of them you can eliminate the more likely you are to avoid error.

Aquinas wanted to be a good empiricist and was well aware of the connection between empiricism and the principle of simplicity. In fact, in the following passage, he considers the principle of simplicity as an objection against his proof of the existence of God.

THE SIMPLICITY OBJECTION

Someone might object that what can be explained by a few principles should not be explained by more. But it seems everything we find in the world can be explained by other principles on the supposition that God does not exist. We can trace natural things back to the principle of their nature, while we trace things that result from purpose back to the principle of human reason or will. There is, then, no necessity for claiming that God exists.

In responding to this objection, it should be said that, since nature functions for a determinate end only under higher direction, it is necessary that the things which come to be by nature are also traced back to God as to a first cause. Likewise, even the things that come to be by purpose have to be traced back to some higher cause beyond human reason or will. For all natural things, including human beings, are changeable and subject to failure and everything changeable and subject to failure must be traced back to a first principle that is not changeable but rather necessary through itself.

Aquinas maintains that natural necessity is not enough. He does not see the principle of simplicity as preventing him from adding divine purpose to the explanation.

Aquinas's justification for this move is that, although nature could function without divine purpose, it could not function for a determinate end without divine purpose. The determinate end supplies us with a standard by which we can assess change and failure. Sometimes nature falls short of reproducing reliable patterns. For example, we may say that an animal's teeth are sharp in front and flat at the back due to natural necessity. Nevertheless, it sometimes happens that an animal is born with deformed teeth or no teeth at all. We have no basis for deeming this a deformity unless we have a notion of how the animal was supposed to be. The notion of 'supposed to be' can only be derived from purpose. If we stick to a naturalistic explanation alone, any configuration that happens is equally necessary. So, while natural necessity alone provides a minimal explanation, natural necessity plus purpose provides a much richer and more powerful explanation. Aquinas feels justified in preferring it for this reason.

Ockham had a colleague named Walter Chatton who also opposed Ockham's use of the principle of simplicity. Chatton developed a counter-principle that has come to be known as Chatton's anti-razor. It states that if one makes a true statement about something that actually exists and two things do not suffice for its verification while another thing is lacking, then one must posit that other thing. So, for example, suppose we have before us a dog born without any teeth and we make the true statement, 'This dog is deformed.' What does it take to verify this statement? The toothless dog and natural necessity are enough only to verify the true statement 'This dog is toothless.' In order to verify the statement that the dog is deformed we need to recognize the standard that the dog fails to achieve. That standard is based on a dog's determinate end that can be supplied only by a designer. According to Chatton's anti-razor, therefore, we must posit divine purpose.

Chatton's anti-razor underlies a common reaction to the teleological argument. Many people are happy to grant that the natural world can be fully explained by the necessity and chance involved in the survival of the fittest. They nevertheless insist that certain aspects of human experience lose their lustre under a strictly naturalistic explanation. For example, we can explain why human beings mate, reproduce, and form family units in purely biological terms without any reference to true love. But who would want to think of something so important in such a reductive way? The notion of true love seems to require a divine purpose that provides a standard against which all of our successes and failures can be measured. Without this divine purpose, life itself seems to lose its meaning.

Ockham may not entirely disagree with this point of view, and perhaps this is why he is happy to confirm the existence of God on faith alone. His only quarrel, a quarrel that persists to this day, is whether it is legitimate to include divine purpose in science.

Creation science

Historians of science have noted the striking similarity between Empedocles's view and the modern theory of evolution by natural selection. This theory is attributed to the nineteenth-century British naturalist Charles Darwin because he was the first to gather the data and construct the theory necessary to make a compelling argument. In his famous work *On the Origin of Species*, Darwin shows how four purely natural factors have produced the complexity we observe in nature:

Replication – Each organism makes copies of itself that live on after its death.

Random Mutation – The copies are never perfect; they contain new traits.

Harsh Conditions – A new trait can provide an advantage for survival.

Eons of Time – Tiny changes in each generation become major changes.

These four factors create a system of evolution by natural selection that keeps the world working all by itself, just like a well-oiled machine. Although each step involves chance, the steps themselves are of necessity so repetitive that they produce predictable results.

According to Darwin, the predictability of the results creates the appearance of purpose. It looks as though teeth were deliberately designed for chewing and eyeballs were deliberately designed for seeing. They look as though they were deliberately designed because they work so well. Darwin insists, however, that if they didn't work so well, they simply wouldn't exist. The natural world ruthlessly eliminates all but the most successful adaptations.

But thinking about the natural world as a well-oiled machine actually brings the question of teleology back into play. Why is it that such a vast and lifeless universe produced conditions ideal for a natural wonder like earth in the first place? Scientists of various different specializations have noticed that the parameters necessary to support the development of advanced life forms are very narrow. If the physical properties and laws of the universe were even minutely different, earth would be just as barren as the other planets.

Consider one small example. In most molecules, the solid form is heavier than the liquid form. Water is the only molecule in which the reverse is true: ice floats. As it turns out, this is a critical fact. If ice did not float, the oceans would freeze from the bottom up, untouched by the sun's melting rays. The earth would now be covered with solid ice, making it entirely uninhabitable.

Dozens of other examples just like this add up to the **anthropic principle**, according to which the conditions in the universe are finely tuned for advanced life forms. How could this be a coincidence?

Some respond to the anthropic principle by pointing out that it is precisely the vastness of the universe that makes life on earth unsurprising. Given a vast, possibly infinite amount of space, and a vast, possibly infinite amount of time, chances are that the right conditions would come together somewhere sometime.

Consider an enormous field of clover. The chance that you would ever find a four-leafer among the multitude of three-leafers is extremely slim. The chance that there is a four-leafer somewhere in there, on the other hand, is actually pretty good. If you happen to be the aphid that was born on that four-leaf clover, you would consider yourself lucky. But if every clover has at least one aphid, then some aphid or other has to be the lucky one. The same logic applies to winning the lottery. The chances that *someone* will win are 100 per cent, while the chances that *you* will win are some tiny fraction of a percentage.

Critics of teleology apply the same logic to our place in the universe. Even though the chance that a place with exactly earth's specifications would evolve is as slim as can be, the chance that some kind of conditions would be right for some kind of life at some point in time may be close to 100 per cent. Moreover, if you happen to be able to conceive of the teleological argument, the chance that intelligent life has evolved in the universe is 100 per cent.

Ongoing debates over the anthropic principle play into the larger question of whether intelligent design should be treated as a theory on equal footing with evolution by natural selection. Some, following in the footsteps of Aquinas, are happy to include teleology as a legitimate part of science. Others, following in the footsteps of Ockham, wish to keep science free of teleology, confining speculation about intelligent design to religious contexts. The medievals still have a great deal of light to shed on this debate.

7

Universals

It is by doubting that we come to investigate,
and by investigating that we recognize the truth.
Peter Abelard

The early middle ages were not a good time for experimentation in Europe. As the years wore on, however, medieval intellectuals were increasingly curious about subjects we now call 'science' – such as biology, zoology, botany, geology, physics, etc. They called these studies of the external world 'philosophy of nature.' Although Aristotle had made great strides in the philosophy of nature, his work was largely unknown in medieval Europe until around 1200. Before then, people knew only that Aristotle organized the study of nature into a system of categories called 'species.' These categories are so effective that we still use them today. Nevertheless, deeper thought about categorizing nature leads to one of the most perplexing problems in philosophy.

The problem of universals

The idea behind the species system is to generate a schema that identifies organisms with similar characteristics and shows how they differ from other organisms. A partial outline of Aristotle's schema is shown overleaf.

Although there were many inaccuracies in the details of Aristotle's schema, the idea of defining the species of an organism became fundamental to the progress of science. We study

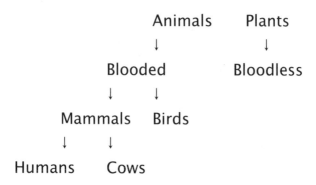

individual members of a species in order to draw conclusions about the species as a whole.

For example, every time we feed a foxglove plant to a cow, the cow dies. This enables us to conclude something about the nature of foxglove, namely, that it is poisonous. If we did our study correctly, then we know not only that the batch of foxglove we tested is poisonous, but also that any batch of foxglove will be poisonous. This is to say that we didn't just learn a property of the single individuals examined; rather, we learned a property of the species itself. So, suppose we grow a completely new batch of foxglove. We have never seen these individual plants before. Yet we already know something about them.

While medieval philosophers accepted the need for a system like Aristotle's, they struggled to explain how we acquire knowledge of a species.

They asked: How can we already know something about individual foxglove plants that we have never seen before?

It's tempting to respond, 'Because these plants are the same as the ones you tested!'

But think about that assertion: 'these plants are *the same* as the ones you tested.' It's not true. They are not the same. This is a completely new batch.

'Well, alright then – they aren't the same individual plants, but they are the same kind of thing.'

This response pinpoints the problem precisely: what exactly is it that makes two different individuals members of the same kind? This question is known as the **problem of universals**, because 'universal' is the philosophical term for 'kind' or 'category.'

Human beings categorize the entire world into kinds of things – plants, cows, raindrops, triangles, peaches, vehicles, etc. When you encounter a particular thing – X – you have to know its universal in order to be able even to register what it is – X is a cup. But where do these universals come from? Are they out in the world to be discovered by us or do our minds impose them on the world?

Being an empiricist, Aristotle wanted to maintain that human beings discover universals in the external world through observation. He asserts that two different individuals are members of the same kind when they have the same essential substance. So when we examine a new batch of foxglove, it isn't entirely new after all. The very same essential substance we examined in the old batch is present in the new batch. Aristotle's solution to the problem of universals is called **immanent realism** because it asserts that the essential substance of each species really dwells within each of its members.

There is a problem with considering immanent realism empiricist, however, because essential substance is not a physical component like a leaf or a root. It can't be seen, heard, tasted, touched, or smelled. According to empiricists all knowledge comes through the five senses. How therefore can we know about essential substance?

Although Aristotle never completely solved this problem, many immanent realists came to consider essential substance as a metaphysical component, like a spirit, that we perceive indirectly. This idea is most easily understood in the case of human beings. We all share the essential substance of humanity, making us 'one in spirit.'

Because immanent realism ultimately relies more on reasoning than on observation, it appealed to innatist philosophers. Consider, for example, how immanent realism could help to justify Augustine's claim, seen in chapter 3, that human beings are responsible for each others' sins. When one of us sins, we all sin, because we all share the same essential substance, humanity. Consider also how immanent realism could support the great chain of being, as seen in chapter 2. Your position on the cosmic hierarchy is determined by the value of the essential substance you share with the members of your species. Immanent realism was the dominant view throughout the middle ages because it complemented so many of the central ideas of medieval Christianity.

Abelard's criticism of immanent realism

Peter Abelard was one of the first philosophers to launch a serious challenge against immanent realism. Abelard argues that immanent realism is incoherent because it is impossible for a single essential substance to be contained within separate individuals.

Take the case of the human species. Either there is just one essential human substance, in which case there is just one human being, or there are many human beings, in which case there are many essential human substances. In other words, each individual thing has to have its own essential substance or it wouldn't be anything at all. According to Abelard, immanent realism is the result of sloppy logic.

PETER ABELARD 1079–1142

Abelard was born into a noble family in northern France. He gave up his title and inheritance, however, in order to become a philosopher. After attending various schools, he became a teacher and was soon famous far and wide for his fearless intellect.

In addition to challenging dominant views in metaphysics and logic, he developed a unique view of ethics, according to which the morality of an action lies in the intention alone. This view was the beginning of the troubles that he wrote about in his autobiography, *The History of My Calamities.*

Abelard fell in love with a beautiful and unusually well-educated girl named Heloise. He arranged to become her private tutor and soon the couple bore an illegitimate son, Astrolabe. When Heloise's guardian found out about the affair, he grounded her and sent thugs to castrate Abelard. The couple defended their intentions in a series of famous love letters.

Abelard became a monk and was able to continue teaching and writing off and on, still persecuted for his radical views.

Abelard boldly presents argument after argument against immanent realism. You will find one of his best in the passage below from a work called *Logic for Beginners*.

CRITIQUE OF IMMANENT REALISM

Immanent realists understand a universal to be a shared essential substance within particular individuals. This essential substance is supposed to be one, but also many, in so far as it is distributed throughout the individuals. Since individuals have a common substance as their essence they are separate from one another only by the differences in their superficial forms. If these superficial forms should be removed there would be utterly no differences between the individuals.

For example, separate human beings share the same essential substance of humanity. Over here humanity is made

Plato by a certain height, weight, and colouring; over there, humanity is made Socrates by a different height, weight, and colouring.

Likewise, according to immanent realism, separate animals of different species have the same essential substance of animality. Animality is drawn into different species by means of different superficial forms. Immanent realists explain their view using the following analogy. I can make one and the same lump of wax into a statue of a human being and into a statue of a cow by pouring it into different forms.

I argue, however, that this analogy doesn't work because of a difference between wax and essential substance. While the same lump of wax does not make up both of the statues at the same time, the same essential substance does make up both of the animals at the same time. At least this is what the immanent realists claim. On their view, the essential substance animality has to be common to all animals in such a way that each animal holds the complete essence equally. If each animal held only part of the essence then they would not be essentially the same, which was the whole point!

Although the authorities seem to support immanent realism, I argue that it contradicts natural knowledge in every way. Here's proof:

1. If Socrates and Brunellus are both animals, then they are essentially the same.

2. Socrates and Brunellus are both animals.

3. So, Socrates and Brunellus are essentially the same.

4. But Socrates, being a man, is essentially rational.

5. And Brunellus, being a cow, is essentially irrational.

---

6. Therefore, rationality is essentially the same as irrationality.

Since this conclusion is absurd, immanent realism must be false.

In this passage, Abelard presents a syllogism for the immanent realists. He feels they are committed to all five premises. Since these premises imply the conclusion, they are committed to the conclusion as well. But the conclusion is a contradiction. In order to avoid this contradiction, immanent realists will have to reject one of the premises, which will be hard to do without causing further problems.

Abelard also represents immanent realism through an analogy. We can reconstruct it in valid form as follows:

1. Wax is to two different statues as essential substance is to two different members of the same genus.

2. The same wax is contained in each statue.

---

3. Therefore, the same essential substance is contained in each genus member.

This analogy makes immanent realism seem intuitively plausible.

But Abelard objects to premise (2). It is not true that the exact same lump of wax goes into each statue. On the contrary, once you put your lump of wax into the cow statue, you can't put it into the human statue. You either have to melt the statue down and start over again or get yourself a second lump of wax.

The immanent realists may reply that if you start with a big enough lump of wax, you can put a part of it into each statue. In saying this, they imply that only a part of the essential substance of animality goes into each animal.

Abelard insists, however, that this defeats the purpose. The purpose was to explain how we can know that this new batch of foxglove will be just as poisonous as the last batch. If the two batches contain different parts of the essential substance, then they may not have the same properties. After all, different parts of the same large lump of wax can have different properties. One part might be grainier, or stickier, or a darker colour than the other part. This difference will cause differences in the two statues made from it. Likewise, if two parts of the essential substance of foxglove can have different properties, then individual batches containing the parts can have different properties. Under these circumstances, how can we claim to know for sure that the new batch of foxglove will be just as poisonous as the last? If the purpose of immanent realism was to secure knowledge, it seems to have failed.

Abelard's nominalism

Abelard presents an alternative to immanent realism called 'nominalism' from the Latin word '*nomina*,' meaning name. **Nominalism** holds that what makes different individuals members of the same kind is nothing but a name. There is no essential substance out there in the world for us to observe. Rather, we impose categories onto things in the world simply by naming them. The name for each universal kind of thing is a universal noun.

In the following passage from another text on logic Abelard argues that immanent realists are mistaken to suppose that universal nouns refer to essential substances.

THE LOGIC OF UNIVERSAL NOUNS

It is often asked, what things do universal nouns refer to? When you hear the universal noun 'humanity,' which is common to all humans, what does it make you think of? If you answer, as you must, that it makes you think of humanity itself, then another question follows: How can you think of humanity itself without thinking of this or that singular human or group of humans?

Consider the case of observation. When you observe humanity with your senses, it is necessary that you observe this or that singular human or group of humans. So, you might suppose that thought works the same way: if you think of humanity, it would be necessary for you to think of this or that singular human or group of humans.

But this analogy is incorrect. Thinking is not like observing. On the contrary, it is more like wanting.

Suppose I say, 'I want something,' and you ask, 'What do you want?' It would be perfectly proper for me to answer, 'A golden castle,' even though there is no such thing as a golden castle. When I said, 'I want something,' I meant I had a certain type of desire, not that the object of my desire actually exists. Likewise, when I say 'I'm thinking of humanity,' I mean I'm having a certain type of thought, not that the object of my thought actually exists.

Things always both agree and differ among themselves. In order to produce knowledge, we invent words to signify the agreement as well as the difference of things. Suppose you want to show that something belongs to or is absent from all humans. You can't do this by referring to a singular instance, like Socrates. The reason is that Socrates is just one human who came and went. Nor can you single out the entire group of humans, because this would take forever. Instead, you speak of 'humanity.' It is necessary to invent universal nouns like 'humanity' to do what singular nouns cannot do.

In this way, knowing is like wanting and not like observing. If no golden castles exist, I cannot truly say, 'I observe a golden castle.' Nevertheless, I can truly say, 'I want a golden castle.' Likewise, I can truly say, 'I have knowledge of humanity' even when there is no such thing as humanity.

Needless to say, people were shocked by Abelard's assertion that there is no such thing as humanity. They thought his nominalism would make natural philosophy impossible and that it would undermine other beliefs and values.

Abelard uses an analogy of his own to make his case. We can reconstruct it as follows:

1. Wanting is to a golden castle as thinking is to universals.
2. You can want a golden castle even though it doesn't exist.

---

3. Therefore, you can think about universals even though they don't exist.

Abelard's point is to show that just because we use the word 'humanity' doesn't mean it corresponds to something really present in the world. The word 'humanity' is just the expression of a certain kind of thought: a thought that divides the world into groups.

The question arises, therefore, how do we distinguish between real objects of knowledge and imaginary objects? In the case of wanting, it doesn't matter whether or not the object is real. But in the case of thinking it does. This indicates a problem with Abelard's analogy. A child might put a banana, a teddy bear, and a clod of dirt into a group and call it 'snickernibs.' Well, obviously, 'snickernibs' is not a true universal noun, and the group it refers to is not a real universal kind. How do we know whether our categories are any more real?

Recognizing that he needed something to distinguish true categories, like humanity, from false categories, like snickernibs, Abelard introduces the notion of a **metaphysical status**. Human beings are all really members of the same group because they share the metaphysical status of humanity. A banana, a teddy bear, and a clod of dirt are not really members of the same group because they do not share any metaphysical status.

A metaphysical status is different from a common essential substance because it does not exist as a thing in the world. Consider a political status, like the presidency. The presidency is not a thing but a role that comes with certain powers. Likewise, human beings share a status that explains how we do what we do while foxgloves share a different status that explains how they do what they do.

While a metaphysical status is not a thing in the world, you still cannot create a metaphysical status by fiat. The presidency is established by a citizen vote. What establishes a metaphysical status? Abelard's answer is God. Metaphysical statuses are abstract ideas in the divine mind that God used as perfect exemplars to create the world. This is what makes them real without actually existing in things.

So, in the end, Abelard relies on a very Platonic picture to secure the reality of our categories. In chapter 1, we witnessed Plato arguing that God used perfect exemplars to create the world. Neoplatonists like Augustine interpreted these perfect exemplars as ideas in the divine mind and used them to guarantee the reality of the categories. The notion that the categories are ideas in the divine mind is considered a version of realism. While Aristotle's version of realism is called 'immanent realism' because it asserts that universals dwell within objects in the physical world, Plato's version of realism is called '**transcendent realism**' because it asserts that universals exist in a realm beyond the physical world. Abelard's nominalism led him straight into transcendent realism!

As the middle ages continued, medieval philosophers were increasingly determined to move away from the neoplatonism that had dominated for so long. So they faced the question: Is there a way to avoid the logical difficulties Abelard adduced for immanent realism without reverting to transcendent realism?

Scotus's acount of universals

John Duns Scotus was an empiricist with an ingenious proposal for a version of immanent realism that avoids the logical difficulties Abelard pointed out.

Recall the syllogism Abelard advances against the immanent realists, above. It asserts that, if Socrates and Brunellus are essentially the same, as immanent realism claims, then rationality and irrationality are essentially the same, which is impossible. Scotus reasoned that if he could find a new interpretation of what it means to be 'essentially the same' he could escape Abelard's conclusion.

The passage below comes from Scotus's *Commentary on the Sentences* in which he carves out his compromise between immanent and transcendent realism.

METAPHYSICAL UNITY

I say that a material substance is not a particular *this* by its own nature. If it were, you would not be able to think of it in universal terms. Universal and particular are opposite characteristics. It's not possible to think about something through its opposite.

There is a real unity in things, apart from all thought, which is less than the numerical unity of a particular. This unity belongs to a nature in virtue of itself. It makes the nature neutral between universal and particular. Therefore, the nature is not of itself one by the numerical unity of a particular. Of itself it is one only by metaphysical unity.

For example, horseness is just horseness; it is neither one nor many, neither universal nor particular. It is not of itself one by a numerical unity any more than it is many by a plurality opposed to that unity. It is not actually universal in the way that something is universal when it is an object of the intellect, nor is it a particular *this* like all of the things we see in the world. For, although it is never really apart from a universal or a particular, of itself, it is not either of them, but rather is naturally prior to them both.

In virtue of its natural priority, this unity is what something is. By itself it is an object of the intellect and by itself as such it is studied by the metaphysician and is expressed through a definition.

But not only is the nature itself of itself indifferent to being in the intellect and in the particular and consequently to being universal or particular, but also, when it has being in the intellect it does not have universality primarily in virtue of itself. For although it is thought of under universality as under a mode of thought, still universality is not part of its primary concept, because universality is not a metaphysician's concept but a logician's.

The unity Scotus posits in this passage is a new kind of essential sameness. Although it is not directly observable, it is metaphysically real.

Scotus intends for his metaphysical unity to provide a real basis for the categories. On the one hand, he insists the metaphysical unity is not itself universal. This would make it into something that our minds impose upon the world, which would amount to Abelard's view. On the other hand, Scotus also insists that it is not itself particular. This would make it the opposite of a universal and hence impossible to categorize. The unity is a real thing that exists in the world but is still categorizable due to its metaphysical nature.

Scotus keeps his metaphysical unity from reducing to an imaginary concept in the mind by asserting that it 'belongs to a nature in virtue of itself.' By this he means that things have this unity independently of thought. Even if no one existed to think about objects in the world, objects in the world would still have it. But how will Scotus keep his unity from reducing to a particular? He asserts that it 'does not have the unity of a particular.' Rather, it has a unity which is 'less than' the unity of a particular. What does he mean by this?

The unity of a particular is also known as numerical identity. Anything that is countable as a single individual has numerical

JOHN DUNS SCOTUS c. 1265–1308

John Duns Scotus may have been born in the town of Duns, which is ten miles north of England. He was presumably called Scotus, meaning "the Scott," due to his Scottish heritage.

Scotus joined the Franciscan monastic order and eventually earned a degree in theology at the University of Oxford. He went on to teach at the University of Paris. While there, he became involved in a controversy between the pope and the king of France. Because he and some other friars sided with the pope in the dispute, they were expelled from France for nearly a year. After his return, Scotus rose to a prestigious position in the university before being transferred to the University of Cologne a few years later.

Scotus's nickname is 'the Subtle Doctor' because he was known to think of ingenious but complicated solutions to philosophical problems. He attracted a good number of followers, who became known as 'scotists.' Although the Catholic Church never canonized him as a saint, they did grant him the status 'blessed.'

identity. For example, one mushroom is a single individual, so it has the unity of a particular. A heap of mushrooms, in contrast, is not a single individual but rather a group of individuals. The heap does not have the unity of a particular. Even though we can loosely call it 'one heap' it's not really a unity at all. It is a plurality.

The unity Scotus introduces in the passage on page 138 is less than the unity of a particular but more than the unity of a heap. In other words, he is trying to suggest that there is a state in between pure identity and pure plurality. The in-between state is the level of unity he calls 'metaphysical unity.' Scotus needs to establish this compromise in order to avoid the problem Abelard detected in immanent realism.

To be essentially the same is to share unity. Abelard therefore assumed that Socrates and Brunellus must share the unity of a particular. This, in turn, means they have everything in common, which is impossible, since one is rational and the other is irrational. Scotus challenges Abelard's assumption by insisting instead that Socrates and Brunellus share the lesser metaphysical unity of animality. But this doesn't mean they have everything in common. Animality is by virtue of its nature neutral to rationality and irrationality. It becomes rational only within some particular material substances, namely, human beings. Since Brunellus is not a human being, animality does not become rational in him. In this way, Scotus's solution blocks the transitivity of essential sameness in Abelard's syllogism.

The key to Scotus's solution is to avoid thinking of the metaphysical unity among members of a kind as though it were a particular. Scotus thinks that a metaphysical unity only becomes a particular by adding particularity, which Scotus famously calls *haecceitas*, meaning 'thisness' in Latin. Scotus's analysis shows what goes wrong in the wax analogy Abelard attacked. Since any wax we observe in the world is already a *this,* it has the unity of a particular; it can't give us a good idea of how metaphysical unity works.

Ockham's nominalism

Scotus's solution to the problem of universals was celebrated in some quarters and criticized in others. One of the leading critics was his fellow Franciscan, William of Ockham. Ockham wanted to adopt whichever account of the categories is most conducive to pure empiricism. After weighing Abelard's nominalism against Scotus's immanent realism, he decided that the former held greater promise than the latter.

According to empiricism, all knowledge comes from observation of the external world. Scotus attempts to secure the reality of our categories by positing a metaphysical unity that is less than pure identity but more than plurality. Abelard, in contrast, attempts to secure the reality of categories by positing a metaphysical status within the divine mind. Which is more empiricist? Neither Scotus's metaphysical unity nor Abelard's metaphysical status can be observed. But Abelard's original system of mental categories can be observed introspectively. Ockham resolved therefore to adopt Abelard's original nominalism, stripped of its metaphysical statuses.

When empiricists assert that knowledge comes from experience, they have to grant that the human mind is itself an object of experience. Recall from chapter 3 that Peter John Olivi argued that if we experience freedom within our own minds then we know it exists. In parallel fashion, Ockham argues that if we experience a system of categories within our own minds, then we know it exists. In Ockham's view, we don't need a metaphysical unity or a metaphysical status to guarantee the reality of our categories. We know which categories are real and which ones aren't by introspectively observing the power of thought itself.

Ockham never directly mentions Abelard, perhaps because Abelard had been condemned by the Church. He does, however, offer long, detailed criticisms of Scotus and other realists. While many of his arguments hinge on the claim that realism is incoherent, we see that one of his underlying concerns is that philosophers cannot be allowed to invent metaphysical entities to solve philosophical problems.

In the passage below, taken from Ockham's *Quodlibetal Questions* and *Summa Logicae*, Ockham contends that, once you acknowledge the power of human thought, there is no need to invent metaphysical entities.

AGAINST METAPHYSICAL INVENTIONS

When we verify a statement about things, if two things suffice for the truth of the statement, then it is redundant to posit another third thing. Consider the following statements:

'A human being is thought of.'

'A human being is the subject of a sentence.'

'A human being is a species.'

It is because of statements like these that philosophers invent metaphysical entities. But two true and really existing things suffice to verify these statements, namely a human being and a mind thinking about that human being. Therefore, there is no need to posit a third thing.

My thesis is evident, for, given there is knowledge of a human being in the mind, it is impossible that this statement is false: 'A human being is thought of.' Likewise, given the concept of human being in general and the concept of subject in general, once this thought is formed: *A human being is the subject of a sentence*, the corresponding statement is true, without there being any invented entity. And likewise for the rest.

Therefore, I say that all categories are truly acts of thinking because these acts of thinking accomplish everything that needs to be accomplished without the need for anything else.

Any view that posits something between the act of thought and the object itself leads to a limitless multiplication of entities:

– a horse is a horse by horseness,

– God is good by goodness, just by justice, and mighty by might,

– a subject is subjected by subjection,

– the apt is apt by aptitude,

– a chimera is nothing by nothingness,

– a blind person is blind by blindness,

– a body is mobile by mobility.

And so on ad infinitum! So we end up multiplying beings according to the multiplicity of terms, which is erroneous and leads us far away from the truth.

Notice that Ockham's arguments in this passage hinge on the principle of simplicity, which we discussed in the previous chapter. Ockham makes a case for his version of nominalism on the grounds that it is simpler than any version of realism, be it transcendent, immanent, or a something between the two.

Ockham's argument can be reconstructed in valid form as follows:

1. A view that multiplies entities without necessity is less likely to be true than a view that doesn't.

2. Any version of realism multiplies entities without necessity while nominalism doesn't.

------

3. Any version of realism is less likely to be true than nominalism.

Realists, of course, do not see their entities as unnecessary at all. They see these entities as necessary to guarantee the reality of our categories. How can thought guarantee the reality of our categories by itself?

In Ockham's view, the world is filled with a multitude of particular individuals that are related to each other through degrees of similarity. This similarity is enough to cause true categorization in the mind. For example, a foxglove is more like a tulip than it is like a human being. This is why we include both the foxglove and the tulip under the universal noun 'plant.' We do not include Socrates under this noun because he is not similarly related.

Relations of similarity become very complicated very quickly. For example, although the foxglove and the tulip are both plants, the foxglove is poisonous while the tulip is not. So every category has subcategories, and every subcategory has further subcategories.

According to Ockham, all of our knowledge comes from observing similarities that cause true categorization in the mind. We can tell true categorizations from false or imaginary ones by introspectively observing them. Any rational adult who compares the idea of humanity to the idea of snickernibs will be able to see that the former comes from real similarities while the latter doesn't. Ockham concludes that, unless you somehow observe a metaphysical status or a metaphysical unity, there is no reason to believe they exist.

Needless to say, however, Ockham did not convince everyone. Immanent and transcendent realism continue to be popular to this day for many reasons. Some realists reject the principle of simplicity. Others accept the principle while denying that thought and the similarity among objects are alone enough to distinguish true categories from false categories. The debate continues. Meanwhile, there is no doubt that nominalism has far-reaching implications across the board in philosophy, as we shall see in the next chapter.

8

Ethics

> Love takes up where knowledge leaves off.
>
> Thomas Aquinas

Around the year 1200 two important factors turned up the heat for the intellectual climate in Europe. The first is that the schools the Catholic Church had maintained for the purpose of training priests began to evolve into universities. What makes a university distinctive is that it grants professional degrees that are recognized everywhere. Because of this universal character, universities adopt similar requirements and curricula.

The second factor is that the works of Aristotle were rediscovered. This second factor is closely connected to the first because Aristotle became a central part of the standard curriculum within the new universities. On the one hand, many of Aristotle's ideas were consistent with Christianity and helped to explain them more clearly. On the other hand, many of his ideas challenged or blatantly contradicted Church teachings. This led to a great deal of controversy. While the controversy was sometimes unpleasant, it slowly became apparent that controversy is necessary for intellectual advancement. Not surprisingly, therefore, controversy has been an integral part of university culture ever since.

William of Ockham is a prime example of someone who provoked university conflict. An enthusiastic empiricist, he was much less willing than others to interpret Aristotle in a way consistent with Catholic teachings. His nominalism, which we examined in the last chapter, provoked the heresy investigation that ultimately destroyed his university career.

The Church's official account of what happens during communion, when bread is miraculously transformed into the body of Jesus, depended on immanent realism. According to the Church's official account, the reason the bread still looks the same after it becomes the body of Jesus is because the 'oneness' of the bread continues to exist. Ockham's rejection of this immanent quantity was interpreted as a rejection of this miracle.

While insisting that a nominalist interpretation of Aristotle could accommodate any miracle the Church required, Ockham refused to change his views. Because of his unfaltering challenge to Church authority, Ockham is considered one of the major forces that brought about the end of the middle ages.

Nominalism also spurred Ockham to go head to head with Thomas Aquinas on ethical theory. The issue between them begins with the Euthyphro question.

The Euthyphro question

The Euthyphro question is of pressing concern for anyone who wants to develop a theory of ethics in conjunction with belief in the existence of God. The question was first posed by Plato in a dialogue named '*The Euthyphro*,' after its central character. The **Euthyphro question** is this: Is a right act right because God commands it, or does God command it because it's right?

This question attempts to ascertain the relationship between God and morality. Is morality derived from God's commands? Or does God make his commands in accordance with morality? It is tempting for theists to answer 'yes' to both questions. On closer examination, however, it is evident that the two options are mutually exclusive: they cannot both be true.

On the one hand, suppose morality is derived from God's commands. This implies that there is no morality without God.

Morality comes about as a result of whatever God decides to require of us.

On the other hand, suppose God makes his commands in accordance with morality. This implies that morality exists independently of God. God's commands merely clarify pre-existing requirements.

By far the most common answer to the Euthyphro question is the second, namely, that morality exists independently of God. This answer has several advantages. First of all, it explains how someone could be moral even though she has no belief in God. Second, it makes it possible for people of different religions to agree about morality even when they cannot agree about God. Third, it makes morality accessible through reason instead of just through divine revelation. This gives us a basis for interpreting revelation and gives everyone an equal claim to knowing the difference between right and wrong.

It seems that the only disadvantage of the second answer is that it puts a constraint on God: God cannot command whatever he wants. He is himself subject to the rules.

Aquinas's natural law theory

Thomas Aquinas unhesitatingly adopts the second answer to the Euthyphro question, convinced that he can overcome its apparent disadvantage. In his view, moral rules do not constrain God because, by nature, God would never want to command otherwise anyway.

Aquinas develops an account of ethics that has come to be known as natural law theory. **Natural law theory** holds that the moral rules are written in nature because God made the world in accordance with them. Human beings can discover the difference between right and wrong by observing the world, including their own nature. Because of its claim that knowledge

THE SUMMA THEOLOGICA (1265–74)

The *Summa Theologica* is Aquinas's greatest work. The title means 'summary of theology,' which appropriately reflects Aquinas's theocentric approach to philosophy. The work spans dozens of volumes and is divided into organized articles on many different topics.

Renaissance philosophers often ridiculed medieval philosophers for speculating about abstruse questions such as 'How many angels can dance on the head of a pin?' Questions such as these make for excellent thought experiments, however, that led medieval philosophers to sophisticated ideas about the nature of reality.

Aquinas devotes a lengthy section of his *Summa* to angels. His official nickname is 'the Angelic Doctor,' partly because of his angelology and partly because he was prone to ecstatic visions. Several months before his death he had a particularly strong ecstatic vision. Thereafter, he refused to write another word, claiming that the vision made all of his work seem like nothing but straw.

of right and wrong requires experience, natural law theory can be considered an empiricist theory.

In fact, we can understand natural law theory more completely with some background in Aristotle's account of human nature, which is based on his **doctrine of the four causes**. According to Aristotle, everything that exists can be explained and every explanation requires answering four questions that roughly correspond to: who? what? why? and how?

Suppose, for example, an alien from outer space is visiting earth and you have been assigned to host his visit. This alien is from a very strange planet where everything is different from earth and so he doesn't understand anything about us. As you begin your tour, the alien points to a house with a puzzled look on his face. According to Aristotle, in order to give an adequate explanation of the house, you will need to address its four causes:

1. The 'efficient' cause (Who made it?) A carpenter
2. The 'material' cause (What is it made of?) Stone and wood
3. The 'final' cause (Why does it exist?) To provide shelter
4. The 'formal' cause (How does it exist?) By enclosing space

Aristotle challenges himself to explain everything in terms of all four causes. This leads him to a very insightful account of human nature. If the alien were to point to a human being with a puzzled look on his face you would need to provide a fourfold explanation. The material and efficient causes of human beings are fairly easy: we are bodies of flesh and blood made by our parents. The formal and the final causes, however, are trickier. After extended analysis, Aristotle concludes that human beings exist to be happy by using reason.

Aristotle determines the final cause of human beings, happiness, through observation. Ask anyone on the street why he is doing what he is doing. He might say he is going to work in order to earn money in order to buy a house in order to support a family. But if you keep pressing, you will eventually come to the ultimate answer to why any human ever does anything: he wants to be happy. Aristotle ascertains that reason is how we accomplish this end by noticing that everything on earth seems to have its own role to play *sub species aeternitatis* (in the grand scheme of things). Human beings are the only animals that can reason. It must be therefore that this is our special function. Reason is how we live a distinctively human life.

So Aquinas's ethics, in following Aristotle's account of human nature, features reason as the primary source of knowledge of right and wrong. By emphasizing reason, Aquinas moderates his empiricism. Although he would never recommend disregarding experience of the external world as Plato would, his ethical theory depends on alleged a priori truths in a way that an extreme empiricist like Ockham would never allow.

The following passage from the *Summa Theologica* contains the crux of Aquinas's ethics.

NATURAL LAW

A statement is called 'self-evident' if its subject logically implies its predicate. If you don't know the definition of the subject, however, the statement won't be self-evident to you. For instance, the statement, 'Man is a rational being,' is self-evident, since whoever says 'man,' by definition, says 'a rational being.' Yet if you don't happen to know that definition, the statement will not be self-evident to you.

Boethius confirms that certain statements are self-evident to everyone who knows the meanings of the words. For example: 'Every whole is greater than each of its parts,' and, 'things equal to one and the same thing are equal to one another.' But some statements are self-evident only to the wise, who understand the meaning of the words involved. For example, to one who understands that an angel does not have a body, it is self-evident that an angel is not circumscriptively in a place. But this is not evident to those who haven't studied the matter.

Rational thought follows a certain order. The notion of 'being' is first, because it is included in absolutely everything we think about. As a result, the first indemonstrable principle of reason is that 'the same thing cannot be affirmed and denied at the same time.' This principle is based on the fact that 'being' and 'not-being' are opposites, as Aristotle affirms.

The notion of 'good' comes second after 'being' because thinking about goodness is required for all action. Everyone acts for an end they conceive of as good. As a result, the second indemonstrable principle of thought is that 'Everyone strives for goodness.' This principle forms a basis for all practical reasoning, which brings us to the topic at hand.

Natural law is based on practical reasoning. Its fundamental principle is that 'good is to be done and pursued and evil is to be avoided.' All other rules of the natural law are based upon this fundamental principle. Whatever one conceives of as good is something to be done. Whatever one conceives of as evil is something to be avoided.

Humans conceive all those things they are naturally inclined toward as good, and consequently as objects to pursue. They conceive the opposite of good as evil and consequently as objects to avoid. Therefore, the rules of natural law follow the order of natural inclinations.

Human beings have three levels of natural inclinations. First, there is the natural inclination we have in common with all living substances. Living substances seek the preservation of their own being. Therefore, it is a rule of natural law to preserve human life and to ward off its obstacles. Second, there is the natural inclination we have in common with other animals. Animals seek to reproduce, educate their offspring, and so forth. Therefore, it is a rule of natural law for human beings to do these things. Third, there is the natural inclination proper to human beings. We alone are able to reason. Therefore, anything dictated by reason is a rule of natural law. For example, reason dictates that we shun ignorance, that we learn the truth about God, and that we live in society without offending those among whom we live.

Aquinas asserts that the principle 'Good is to be done and evil is to be avoided' is an a priori principle that supplies the foundation for ethics. This dash of innatism tempers the empiricism in his natural law theory.

We can reconstruct the main point of this passage in valid form as follows:

1. All things strive after goodness.
2. If all things strive after goodness, then human beings should do good and avoid evil.

3. Doing good and avoiding evil means acting in accordance with natural inclinations.

4. Human beings have three levels of natural inclination:
   i) preserving themselves (like plants)
   ii) preserving their families (like animals)
   iii) preserving their communities (as only humans can).

---

5. Therefore, human beings should preserve themselves, their families, and their communities.

Aquinas is careful to stress that reason must be the guiding principle in correctly following natural inclinations. He justifies this on Aristotelian grounds – that the special function of the human species is reason. We are the only creatures on earth capable of this higher level of agency. Therefore, reason must always trump the lower levels of inclination in the case of conflict.

For example, Aquinas famously defends the possibility of a just war. Although every human being has a natural inclination to preserve himself, it is moral to sacrifice your own life by dying on the battlefield as long as the war is justified. He specifies three conditions for a war to be just: it must be commanded by the rightful sovereign, there must be a just cause, and it must be fought to promote good and to eliminate evil. These three conditions can be interpreted in terms of his third level of natural inclination according to which human beings must use reason to preserve their communities.

Aquinas applies natural law theory to quite a number of concrete examples. This is just as it should be since an ethical theory is meant to help us figure out what to do in various real-life circumstances. The problem is that it is not clear that the theory passes the test for being a workable guide in these circumstances. As a good example, let's look at what Aquinas has to say about drinking.

The following passage also comes from the *Summa Theologica*.

ON DRUNKENNESS

The sin of drunkenness consists in the immoderate use and desire of wine. This may happen to you in three ways. First, you might not know you are drinking too much of an intoxicating beverage. In this case, your drunkenness would be without sin. Second, you may know you're drinking too much of the beverage without knowing it to be intoxicating. In this case, your drunkenness would involve the venial sin of excessive consumption. Third, you might be well aware that you're drinking too much of an intoxicating beverage, and yet you would rather be drunk than abstain from drink. In that case, you're a 'drunkard' properly speaking, because moral labels are applied not due to accidental occurrences, but due to direct intentions. Deliberate drunkenness is a mortal sin, because you willingly and knowingly deprive yourself of the use of reason whereby you perform virtuous deeds and avoid wrongdoing. Thus you sin mortally by running an unacceptable risk.

While careful to concede that getting drunk by accident is excusable, Aquinas clearly asserts that drinking to get drunk on purpose is wrong. In fact, he calls it a 'mortal sin,' which is the worst kind of wrong within Catholicism because it means that if you die before you pray for forgiveness, you will be sent directly to hell. We can see exactly why Aquinas thinks drinking to get drunk is so immoral: it deprives the agent of reason, which is in his view the *sine qua non* of morality and of truly human functioning.

Criticism of Aquinas

Given that drinking to get drunk is a commonplace in our modern society, we should ask whether Aquinas's analysis is plausible. It could be, after all, that modern society is wrong to condone drunkenness. Just because a particular view is popular does not mean it is correct. In fact, this is known as the **fallacy ad populum** – accepting a view because it is widely held without regard to whether or not it is true. Consider the fact that there was a time when it was popular to believe that the earth is flat. The popular view turned out to be wrong. Consider also the fact that slavery was once a popular practice despite its immorality. According to Aquinas, natural law theory prohibits homosexuality, masturbation, extramarital sex, and a whole host of other popular activities. It would be fallacious to assert that his view is incorrect simply because so many people engage in these activities. Popularity is not a good indicator of truth.

Nevertheless, Aquinas's claims are not above criticism and we should pause to see how someone might object to his assessment of drunkenness. There are two main possibilities:

(1) Natural law theory is correct but Aquinas is incorrect to think it implies that drinking to get drunk is severely immoral.

(2) Natural law theory is incorrect.

We should consider each of these possibilities in turn.

Someone may argue for possibility number one on the grounds that it is reasonable to suspend reason on occasion. After all, alcohol is known as the 'social lubricant.' It functions to cement bonds among people who might not otherwise be inclined toward friendship. Since promoting community is the highest level of natural inclination for human beings, drinking to get drunk could be justified as a natural inclination.

Someone might argue for possibility number two on the grounds that morality cannot be derived from reason. Aquinas tells us that morality requires acting in accordance with reason. But how do we know whether a given action is reasonable? Aquinas tells us that acting in accordance with reason means following natural inclinations. But how do we know whether a given action is natural or unnatural?

If we look to the natural world we get conflicting messages. Koala bears are known to intoxicate themselves on fermented berries. Does this show that intoxication is natural and therefore permissible for human beings? Probably not. Animals engage in all kinds of behaviour that would be immoral for human beings. For example, black widow spiders regularly bite the heads off their mates. Some philosophers have criticized natural law theory on the grounds that animal behaviour cannot provide an ethical model for humans. Surely Aquinas never meant for his theory to be interpreted in such simplistic terms, however. To reject natural law theory on this basis may be an instance of the straw man fallacy.

So how do we determine what counts as a natural inclination for human beings? Each human being seems to have different inclinations. Some are inclined toward drunkenness and others are not. In order to substantiate his claim that human nature is a guide for right and wrong, Aquinas needs to assume that human nature is the same for everyone, even if some people are ignorant of the true essence of that nature.

Appealing to a common essence among all the members of a species should sound familiar from the previous chapter. Natural law theory presupposes immanent realism.

Aquinas openly embraces immanent realism despite the problems with it that we discussed in the previous chapter. Dismissing these problems as insignificant, he concludes that if we study the humanity that is within us all we will be able to discern our true natural inclinations.

Ockham's divine command theory

From what we have already seen of Ockham it should be evident that he will hardly be content with Aquinas's conclusion. Ockham's rejection of both immanent and transcendent

THE SUMMA LOGICAE (c. 1320s)

The *Summa Logicae* is Ockham's greatest work. The title means 'summary of logic,' which appropriately reflects Ockham's logocentric approach to philosophy. He seems to have completed the work after he was arrested under suspicion of heresy. Because he was never able to return to university, his official nickname is 'the Venerable Inceptor' – an inceptor being someone who is on the point of earning a degree.

Ockham's *Summa* is primarily an exposition of supposition theory, which is an account of how words refer to things. His version of supposition theory is greatly affected by his nominalism, according to which universal terms do not refer to universal things. Ockham shows how language that appears to refer to universal things can be reinterpreted without making reference to anything other than particular things.

Ockham was convinced that a lot of philosophical problems arise from the misuse and misunderstanding of language.

realism made it impossible for him to accept natural law theory, or any ethical theory that posits a universal standard for morality. On the contrary, Ockham knew he needed to embrace the first answer to the Euthyphro question: Morality is derived from God's commands. This approach to ethics has come to be known as **divine command theory**. God does not count as a universal standard for morality within divine command theory because he can command one thing for one person and a completely different thing for someone else. An ethics based on universal standards, like that of Aquinas, implies that everyone is subject to the same rules.

Divine command theory is problematic because it implies that anything could become moral or immoral. Whatever God commands is right *simpliciter* and there is nothing to prevent God from commanding something that seems wrong to us. For example, consider the famous case from the Old Testament in which God commands Abraham to kill his son Isaac as a sacrifice. Many people interpret this passage in such a way that God never really intended for Abraham to kill Isaac because they can't imagine God commanding such a thing. According to Ockham, however, God can command such a thing.

Ockham makes his case for divine command theory in the following passage taken from his *Commentary on the Sentences*.

RIGHT AND WRONG ARE NOT UNIVERSALS

Hatred, theft, adultery, and the like are evil according to the common law, which is designed to enforce divine commands. As far as everything absolute in these actions is concerned, however, God can perform them without involving any evil. Furthermore, someone on earth would rightly perform them if they should fall under a divine command. Currently it is wrong for people on earth to perform these acts. The reason is that right now the opposite of these acts fall under a divine command.

'Mortal sin' does not have a real essence. For there is no one real thing, whether positive or negative, that it signifies. Therefore, it has only a nominal definition. In other words, it signifies many things that have no unity, either through themselves or through association.

We can say that the definition of 'mortal sin' is this: to commit an act that one was obligated by eternal punishment not to commit or to omit an act that one was obligated by eternal punishment to commit. Therefore, mortal sin is nothing other than to commit or omit some act concerning which God ordained eternal punishment.

From this it is evident that God would not sin by being the total cause of an act that a sinner commits. For God cannot be obligated toward any act. This is why, if God wills something, then it is right, regardless of what it is. Obligation, therefore, is what makes someone a sinner or not a sinner. Suppose God were to be a total cause of a man's hatred. Then neither the man nor God would sin: God not, because he is not obligated toward anyone; the man not, because the hatred would not be in his power.

Ockham's commitment to divine command theory rests squarely on his nominalism. Because there is no universal standard for right and wrong, every case may be different.

Ockham's reasoning can be reconstructed in basic modus tollens form as follows:

1. If the same acts were necessarily always wrong, then they would have a common essence.

2. There is no such thing as a common essence among things.

3. Therefore, the same acts are not necessarily always wrong.

Ockham is making room for unlimited variation in the morality of our actions. In his view, for example, drunkenness might be wrong for some people some of the time, but not for other people or even for the same people at other times.

The first question that arises about this approach to ethics is, how do individual human beings find out what God requires of them? Ockham's answer is that God's commands are revealed in our conscience. This immediately makes Ockham's theory seem innatist since we have to turn within to find the truth rather than observing the world. Ockham's divine command theory is not, however, innatist. It is based on introspection in the same way that his nominalism and his metaphysical libertarianism are based on introspection. When you contemplate an action, your conscience will tell you whether it is right or wrong. We quickly learn through experience that some acts feel right and others feel wrong. Ockham characterizes the feeling of rightness in terms of good will and the feeling of wrongness in terms of bad will. Of course, you can ignore your conscience or be mistaken about it. But this is no different than ignoring or being mistaken about what you see with your own two eyes. Ockham thinks of morality as an especially evident kind of demonstrative science because we have more experience of our own acts than we have of anything else.

Critics of this view, however, complain that it has the effect of undermining morality altogether. If you consult your conscience and genuinely feel it commanding you to do something traditionally considered wrong, then you should do it, according to Ockham. It might be liberating at first to think that there are no absolute moral rules. But do you really trust your own conscience as a reliable guide? And do you trust the conscience of others? Anyone can lie, cheat, steal, and even murder as long as they feel their conscience commanding them to do it. Many terrible crimes have been committed in the name of conscience.

Ockham's view is by far a minority position among philosophers. His willingness to put himself on the line for it is, in part, a testament to his commitment to nominalism. It would be inconsistent for Ockham to resurrect a de-platonized version of Abelard's nominalism against Scotus and then neglect to apply it across the board. If universals don't exist, then they don't exist. Nominalists simply have to accept the implications of their view, whether they like it or not. Nevertheless, the truth is that Ockham actually found divine command theory more intuitively appealing than natural law theory. On further investigation it becomes clear why.

Natural law theory and divine command theory envision two fundamentally different kinds of motivation for morality. The most basic question that arises in ethics, which everyone has to face at some time or other, is this: Why be moral in the first place? It's hard enough to figure out the moral thing to do in many cases, but even when we know perfectly well what we ought to do, we often don't want to do it. On such an occasion one might ask, 'Why should I be moral?' For example, suppose you're walking through a parking lot behind an elderly gentleman. You see him drop a twenty-dollar bill. You pick up the bill and look around. Neither he nor anyone else knows what happened. You could pocket the bill and drive away, twenty dollars richer and no one else the wiser. It seems clear that the right thing would be to return the bill to its owner. But why should you do the right thing? Aquinas and Ockham have very different answers.

According to natural law theory, you should do the right thing because reason requires it. Aquinas would no doubt appeal to his third level of natural inclination in this case and insist that returning the money promotes good community, which reason tells us is the right thing to do. There are other ethical theories throughout the history of philosophy that appeal to reason as the motive for moral behaviour, though in different ways. These theories are called **rationalist** ethical theories.

According to divine command theory, in contrast, you should do the right thing because good will requires it. Ockham would no doubt suggest that your conscience tells you to love your neighbour, and this love, which is really an extension of your love of God, obligates you to return the money. There are other ethical theories throughout the history of philosophy that appeal to love and good will as the motive for moral behaviour, though in different ways. These theories are called **voluntarist**, from the Latin word '*voluntas*,' meaning will.

So, divine command theory makes being good a matter of love more than reason while natural law theory makes being good a matter of reason more than love. Everyone has to make moral decisions. Being a good decision maker means understanding what motivates you. Are you a voluntarist or a rationalist?

Ethics and politics

Here's a thought experiment to demonstrate the difference further. Imagine two ideal societies called Alpha and Beta. Both are clean, peaceful, and productive. The only difference between the two is as follows.

In Alpha, people do the right thing because they are full of good will toward their king. Their king has done great deeds for them and they are so grateful that they would do anything for him. He could make them do anything he wants, but he is so devoted to them that he makes only the most reasonable requests. The Alphans do their duty out of love for him.

In Beta, on the other hand, people do the right thing because they are perfectly rational. Beta has a great king too, but the people of Beta don't do their duty out of gratitude toward him. Rather, they do it because the king's requests always conform to what they consider reasonable anyway. In fact, the Betans often simply figure out sensible laws on their own without regard for what the king wants.

The question for the thought experiment is this: which society would you rather live in? Would you rather live by love or by reason? Ockham would rather live by love, and this is why he welcomes divine command theory as an implication of his nominalism. He thinks Aquinas is putting reason before love and thereby giving people the wrong motive for being good.

Here's another related question: Suppose you come home one day to find that your daughter has cleaned the entire garage. When you ask her why she did it, she could give two different responses: (1) because she loves you, (2) because she could see it needed to be done. Which answer would you rather hear?

Of course, Ockham does carve out a role for reason in his divine command theory. Since it is often difficult to know exactly what God wants, or what our conscience is saying, we have to use reason to figure it out. Likewise, Aquinas leaves room for love in his natural law theory. In fact, being inclined toward compromise, Aquinas would be likely to assert that a truly good person is motivated by both reason and love.

All parties to the dispute agree that living by both love and reason is ideal, but given that reality presents cases of conflict, we have to face the question of which should be decisive.

This question transfers from the ethical domain to the political domain, just as our thought experiment about the Alphans and the Betans suggests. James of Viterbo was an Augustinian monk who lived in the generation between Aquinas and Ockham (1255–1308). In the following passage, he argues that good government requires obedience to the king as well as to the law.

THE BEST PERSON AND THE BEST LAWS

A government is not complete unless both the best person and the best law are present. A human being is needed, first, to inspire observance of the law and second, to supplement the law when there are new cases and exceptions. But the law is also needed, first, to be consistent over long periods of time and second, because no human being is so good that he might never be deceived or corrupted. In fact, there are very few 'best persons' to be found. Therefore, neither law without a human being nor a human being without law is sufficient for good government.

But what if it is necessary to take only one of these two?

If we are speaking about someone who becomes 'best' through natural principles, then it is better to be ruled by the best law. A human being and a law can both be lacking, but there are fewer negative consequences from government by law than by someone who is best by nature. For law works for the majority of cases, whereas, without the grace of God, one can go wrong every which way.

If, on the other hand, we are speaking about someone who becomes 'best' through the infused grace of God, then it is better to be ruled by him. We read about such rulers. Guided by a divine gift, they do not wander from the right path. Meanwhile, the law will always be flawed, unless it has been handed down by God.

It might be objected that human beings are ministers of the law meaning that we serve it, not the other way around. My response is that human beings are also the founders of the law. Human beings animate the law because what pleases a righteous ruler has the force of law.

When it comes to the best person versus the best law, Viterbo is reluctant to give priority to one or the other. But in cases of conflict he asserts that whichever one has a divine source is the clear winner. Hence a king infused with divine grace has priority over ordinary law, while divinely revealed law has priority over an ordinary king. Notice, however, that Viterbo doesn't tell us how to determine whether a human being or a law has a divine source.

In the end, Aquinas and Ockham agree that we have to use reason to interpret divine command and we have to allow divine command to guide reason. Both recognize love and rationality as important parts of the equation. Furthermore, many of their judgments about the morality of a particular action may coincide. Nevertheless, when push comes to shove, Aquinas will side with reason and Ockham will side with love. Although this is a subtle difference, even the subtlest differences in philosophy can make a big difference in how a person sees the world.

Conclusion

Medieval philosophy can be summed up as an era in which Christian, Muslim, and Jewish thinkers undertook to adapt the ideas of the great ancient philosophers to their religion. That is to say, it was a millennium-long exploration of the compatibility – or lack thereof – between faith and reason. In this book, we looked primarily at the Christian adaptation of Plato and Aristotle, focusing on the most important developments that survived beyond the middle ages to the present day.

In chronological order, medieval philosophy proceeds first from intense interest in Plato, second, toward an effort to combine the insights of Plato and Aristotle, and third, toward a strong emphasis on Aristotle. We can see this movement in the three main authors we studied: Augustine, Aquinas, and Ockham.

Augustine stands at the very beginning of the medieval period. Adopting Plato's key idea that the world is modelled on a perfect exemplar, Augustine strives to understand why the world seems so imperfect. In the process, he lays the groundwork for a philosophical topic of enduring interest known as the problem of suffering or the problem of evil: Why do bad things happen to good people? In his effort to solve this problem, Augustine reinforces the concept of the great chain of being, which undergoes its most sophisticated development in Anselm's ontological proof of the existence of God. He also unleashes a whole slew of difficulties surrounding the belief in human freedom, thereby opening the door to Boethius's account of divine foreknowledge as well as two opposing positions that have come to be known as determinism and metaphysical libertarianism. Jean Buridan, representing the former view, argues that free will is an illusion caused by the hesitation of the intellect, while Peter John Olivi, representing the latter view, insists that if human beings lacked free will they would not be responsible for what they do. Despite adding new rigour to the argument, these authors are really just advancing conflicting themes found within Augustine's original work.

Aquinas stands at the height of the medieval period. Enriched by the sudden influx of previously unavailable works of Aristotle, Aquinas endeavours to understand the world in terms of divine purpose rather than divine perfection. Aristotle's conviction that nature always works for the best becomes evidence for Aquinas that God is behind the workings of nature. In pursuing this line of thought, Aquinas articulates the teleological proof of the existence of God. To many, this proof is more convincing than the cosmological proof, which contends, *pace* Averroes and Maimonides, that the world must have had a beginning. Aquinas maintains that nature not only reveals God's existence but also reveals his will. Casting human rationality itself as a part of nature, he argues that we can discover how God wants us to live by reasoning about our own natural inclinations. The resulting view, known as natural law theory, became influential in ethics as well as political theory, as demonstrated by James of Viterbo. Aquinas is paradigmatic of the medieval synthesis of religion and philosophy, faith and reason, precisely because he sees God in nature. Refusing to distance God through transcendence, as mystics like Meister Eckhart were prone to do, Aquinas makes God the centre of every scientific inquiry.

Ockham stands at the end of the medieval period. Though arriving on the scene only a few generations after Aquinas, he undermines the synthesis of faith and reason that culminated in Aquinas, and thereby precipitates the end of the era. Ockham sees no evidence of divine perfection or of divine purpose in the world. Taking Aristotle to a logical extreme, he argues for the principle that has come to be known as Ockham's razor: the simplest explanation is most likely to be true. Science provides the simplest explanation of the natural world without needing to make any reference to God. Therefore, belief in God is a matter of faith alone, not to be proven or combined with scientific investigation. This view, known as fideism, is widely embraced throughout the modern world. What is not so widely recognized, however, is the connection between fideism and nominalism, a view originally defended by Abelard, according to which there is no such thing as universals. Both Augustine's idea of perfection in nature and Aquinas's idea of purpose in nature rely on these unseen metaphysical entities, which even John Duns Scotus attempts to salvage in his own way. It is precisely by refusing to recognize the existence of any such entities that Ockham severs the cord between religion and philosophy.

In this book we have featured the duelling epistemologies of Plato and Aristotle in order to crystallize the difference between them and to carve two recognizable paths through the middle ages.

Plato's innatism prompts us to find truth within while anchoring this truth in a divine source. Augustine and Anselm demonstrate this methodology most clearly in their proofs of the existence of God. They picture the entire world ranked in a hierarchy in perfect proportion beneath the apparent chaos we see on the surface.

Aristotle's empiricist alternative is naturalistic, seeking truth in our experience of the world. It receives its purest expression in Olivi and Ockham, even when their observations concern the workings of the human mind.

Aquinas and Scotus are two authors who stake out a compromise between innatism and empiricism. They both decide that, while the truth is embedded in nature, it is not strictly observable. We have to rely on pure reason about underlying metaphysical structures in order to interpret what we experience.

Of course, the innatist and empiricist paths do not stop at the end of the middle ages. The British empiricists John Locke (1632–1704), George Berkeley (1685–1753), and David Hume (1711–76) carry on where Olivi and Ockham left off, while the continental rationalists René Descartes (1596–1650), Baruch Spinoza (1632–77), and Gottfried Wilhelm Leibniz (1646–1716) take their cue from Augustine and Anselm. Advancing the questions we have examined in new directions as well as adding new ones, these philosophers in turn set the stage for recent developments in philosophy. Just as the medieval philosophers stood on the shoulders of Plato and Aristotle, modern and contemporary philosophers stand on the shoulders of the medievals.

All of us, whether philosophers or not, benefit from medieval discussions of the deep issues surrounding the existence of God. Once you are aware of them, you cannot ignore how much they have shaped who we are.

Post Script

It may be glaringly obvious that no women authors are included in this book. While we have witnessed religious and ethnic diversity through Averroes and Maimonides, we have not sampled any medieval female philosophers. Why?

The short answer is that there simply weren't any. In medieval Europe, education was scarce enough for men and much more so for women. Girls did not typically learn to read, at least not at an advanced level, and they were never allowed in the universities. Therefore, they were not able to contribute to the literary history of the period.

HYPATIA (c. 370–415)

Hypatia was a Greek philosopher and mathematician who taught neoplatonism out of her own home in Alexandria, Egypt. Many prominent pagans and Christians attended her school. She became known far and wide for her intellectual achievements.

Hypatia's status as a woman was a constant challenge for her, however, eventually leading to her demise. There are conflicting accounts of the ostensible reason for the sudden violence against her. Some accused her of black magic. Others accused her of associating with the wrong political party. But just being a learned female in the fifth century was provocation enough. One day when she was in her forties she was ambushed by a mob of Christians, stripped naked, dragged through the streets, stoned, and incinerated. No written work by her survives.

Ceteris paribus, Hypatia would, no doubt, have made the list of great medieval philosophers.

There are, however, some rare exceptions, mostly from the very end of the middle ages. Because intellectual activity was reserved for men, these women had to present themselves as mystics in order to be heard. Their work was accepted only as a message from God.

Hildegard of Bingen (1098–1179) was from a noble German family. Because she was the tenth surviving child, her parents dedicated her at birth to the Church. She wrote about her visions and founded a convent. Birgitta of Sweden (1302–73) was from a noble Swedish family. Though forced to marry at age thirteen, she also wrote about her visions. Catherine of Siena (1347–80) was from a wealthy Italian family. She taught herself to read and wrote letters to the clergy to spread the ideas she received in her visions. She gave sermons as well.

Peter Abelard's lover, Heloïse (1101–62), whom we met in chapter 7, exchanged private letters containing philosophical content.

Needless to say, none of these women was in any position to engage publicly in the philosophical debates we have been discussing in this book. The only one who comes close is Christine Pisan (1364–1430), who was the daughter of the royal astrologer of the French king. He allowed her to be educated like a boy until she was fifteen, at which time she was married. When her husband died young, she supported herself and her family by writing poetry and political theory. Almost all of her work was published after 1400, however, which makes her less of a medieval and more of a renaissance figure.

For further reading on the topic of medieval women writers see Katharina Wilson, *Medieval Women Writers* (Athens, GA: University of Georgia Press, 1984).

Glossary

Accidentally ordered sequence
A sequence in which posterior members do not depend on prior members for their existence.

Actual infinite
A set with infinitely many members.

Anthropic principle
The assertion that conditions in the universe are finely tuned for advanced life forms.

Argument from analogy
A valid argument form that can be schematized as follows:
1. A is to B as C is to D.
2. A is P with respect to B.

3. Therefore, C is P with respect to D.

Argument from introspection
An argument for metaphysical libertarianism based on the alleged experience of being able to select one or the other of two options.

Buridan's ass
A thought experiment used to test our intuitions about free will. While a hungry donkey placed between two equal food sources would starve to death a human being would be able to break the tie.

Category mistake
A sentence that makes an impossible presupposition about its subject.

Compatibilism
A version of determinism according to which being determined to do exactly what we do is compatible with freedom as long as the antecedent conditions that determine what we do include our own choices.

Conditional necessity
According to Boethius, a relationship between two things that does not take away free will. Schematically: Necessarily (If X, then Y).

Conditional statement
An 'if-then' statement. For example: If it is raining, then the streets are wet. The 'if' part is called the 'antecedent' and the 'then' part is called the 'consequent.'

Cosmological proof
An argument for the existence of God based on the alleged need for a first cause of the universe.

Creation model
The view that God created the universe *ex nihilo* some finite number of years ago.

Determinism
The view that human beings do not have free will but rather are determined by antecedent conditions (such as God or nature or environmental factors) to do exactly what they do.

Disjunctive syllogism

A valid argument form that can be schematized as follows:

1. Something is either F or G.
2. x is not F.

—————————

3. Therefore, x is G.

Divine idleness question

What was God doing all by himself for all eternity before he created the universe?

Doctrine of the four causes

According to Aristotle, everything that exists can be explained and every explanation requires answering four questions that roughly correspond to: who? what? why? and how?

Doctrine of illumination

Augustine's Christian version of innatism, according to which God implants and reveals truths within the mind.

Empiricism

The epistemology according to which knowledge comes from observation of the world.

Epistemology

The branch of philosophy that studies the nature of knowledge.

Essentially ordered sequence

A sequence in which the posterior members depend on prior members for their existence.

Eternity

Without beginning or end. According to Boethius, the 'simultaneous and complete possession of infinite life.'

Euthyphro question
Is a right act right because God commands it, or does God command it because it's right?

Evidentialism
The view that faith can be confirmed by reason and evidence.

Fallacy
A mistake in reasoning.

Ad hominem
To attempt to win an argument by discrediting the character or reputation of the opponent.

Ad populum
To accept a view because it is widely held without regard for whether it is true.

Begging the question
To assume the very thing you are trying to prove.

False dilemma
To arbitrarily reduce multiple alternatives to only two.

Straw man
To refute a simplistic substitute for the opponent's argument rather than the argument itself.

Fideism
The view that the truths of religion must be taken on faith alone.

Free will defence
A solution to the problem of suffering according to which God judges that free will is so valuable that it is worth the price of the cruelty that some people choose.

Great chain of being

A cosmic scale according to which the absolute value of every existing thing can be measured.

Great-making characteristic

All of the characteristics that make a being great, such as omniscience, omnibenevolence, and omnipotence.

Hypothetical syllogism

A valid argument form that can be schematized as follows:

1. If something is X, then it is Y.
2. If something is Y, then it is Z.

___

3. Therefore, if something is X, then it is Z.

Immanent realism

The view that the essential substance of each species is really immanent within each of its members.

Innatism

The epistemology according to which knowledge comes from reasoning within the mind. Also called 'rationalism' throughout the history of philosophy.

Metaphysical libertarianism

The view that human beings are responsible for their actions as individuals because they have free will, defined as the ability to do other than they do.

Metaphysical status

Abstract ideas in the divine mind that God used as perfect exemplars to create the world. According to Abelard, makes categories real without actually existing in things.

Metaphysical unity
According to Scotus, an unobservable empirical reality that establishes the categories by being neither universal nor particular.

Modus ponens
A valid argument form that can be schematized as follows:
1. If something is P, then it is Q.
2. x is P.

_____

3. Therefore, x is Q.

Modus tollens
A valid argument form that can be schematized as follows:
1. If something is P, then it is Q.
2. x is not Q.

_____

3. Therefore, x is not P.

Natural law theory
The view that the moral rules are written in nature because God made the world in accordance with them.

Negative theology
The study of God through what may not be said about him.

Neoplatonism
A mystical interpretation of Plato that promotes disdain for the material world.

Nominalism
The view that what makes different individuals members of the same kind is nothing but a name.

Occasionalism

The idea that there is no necessity in the (horizontal) connection between cause and effect because God causes each event vertically.

Ontological proof

An argument for the existence of God based on the nature of being.

Oscillating model

The view that there is no absolute beginning of the universe; it has always existed.

Principle of simplicity

(Ockham's razor) The assertion that the simpler theory is more likely to be true. Alternate formulations: It is futile to do with more what can be done with less. Entities should not be multiplied without necessity.

Problem of divine foreknowledge

How can God know the future without destroying human freedom?

Problem of suffering

Why do bad things happen to good people?

Problem of universals

What exactly is it that makes two different individuals members of the same kind?

Rationalism (in epistemology)

See Innatism.

Rationalism (in ethics)

The view that reason is the motive for moral behaviour.

Reductio ad absurdum
Method of argumentation aiming to show that the opponent's view implies something that cannot possibly be true.

Reformatory conception of justice
The view that the purpose of punishment is to prevent future wrongdoing.

Retributive conception of justice
The view that the purpose of punishment is to make the criminal pay for the crime.

Rhetorical question
A question asked to make a point rather than gain information. Can be very persuasive when used in advertisements; can be manipulative when used in philosophy.

Scholasticism
Method of learning institutionalized by the first universities *c.* 1100–1500, requiring students to examine statements from religion and science that appear to conflict and to show how the conflict could be resolved. The term 'scholastic' has come to mean 'bookwormish.'

Simple necessity
According to Boethius, a requirement of nature that takes away free will.
Schematically: If X, then necessarily Y.

Soundness
The highest praise for an argument. If you judge an argument to be sound, this means you think it is valid and all of its premises are true.

Stoicism

The school of thought founded by Zeno of Citium just before 300 BC, according to which all emotion arises from false judgment and reason is the only path to true freedom.

Teleological proof

An argument for the existence of God based on the design of the world.

Temporal anti-realism

The view that time is dependent on the human mind.

Temporal realism

The view that time exists independently of the way the human mind experiences it.

Transcendent realism

The view that universals exist in a realm beyond the physical world.

Universal

The philosophical term for a category or kind of thing.

Validity

Correct structure for a deductive argument such that the premises logically imply the conclusion. If the premises were true, the conclusion would have to be true. The premises do not, however, have to be true for validity.

Voluntarism

The view that love is the motive for moral behaviour.

Zeno's paradox

The claim that since there are an infinite number of halfway marks between every two points on the road, you will never be able to traverse it.

Further reading

Chapter 1

The passage called 'My Defence' comes from *Plato: Apology*, ed. Harold North Fowler (Cambridge, MA: Harvard University Press, 1917), pp. 80–6. For an English translation of the entire work see *The Last Days of Socrates: Euthyphro; The Apology; Crito; Phaedo*, trans. H. Tarrant and H. Tredennick (Harmondsworth: Penguin Classics, 1993). See also the following site on the Internet: '*Apology* by Plato,' translated by Benjamin Jowett, The Internet Classics Archive, ed. Daniel C. Stevenson, http://classics.mit.edu/Plato/apology.html.

The passage called 'Logic Basics' comes from *Aristotle: Prior Analytics*, ed. Hugh Tredennick (Cambridge, MA: Harvard University Press, 1962), pp. 198–204. For an English translation of the entire work see *Aristotle, Prior Analytics*, trans. R. Smith (Hackett, 1989). See also the following site on the Internet: 'Prior Analytics by Aristotle,' translated by A. J. Jenkinson, The Internet Classics Archive, ed. Daniel C. Stevenson, http://classics.mit.edu/Aristotle/prior.html.

The passage called 'The Best Makes the Best' comes from *Plato: Timaeus*, ed. R. G. Bury (Cambridge, MA: Harvard University Press, 1961), pp. 54–64. For an English translation of the entire work see *Timaeus and Critias*, trans. D. Lee (Harmondsworth: Penguin Classics, 1972). See also the following site on the Internet: '*Timaeus* by Plato,' translated by Benjamin Jowett, The Internet Classics Archive, ed. Daniel C. Stevenson, http://classics.mit.edu/Plato/timaeus.html.

The passage called 'Observations of Motion and Shape' comes from *Aristotle: De caelo*, ed. W. K. C. Guthrie (Cambridge, MA: Harvard University Press, 1953), pp. 218–54. For an English translation of the entire work see *The Works Of Aristotle, vol. 2: Physica, De Caelo And De Generatione Et Corruptione*, trans. W. D. Ross (Kessinger Publishing, 2007). See also the following site on the Internet: '*On the Heavens* by

Aristotle,' translated by J. L. Stocks, The Internet Classics Archive, ed. Daniel C. Stevenson, http://classics.mit.edu/Aristotle/heavens.html.

For a general introduction to ancient logic see J. Corcoran, *Ancient Logic and Its Modern Interpretations* (New York: Springer, 2006) as well as J. Barnes, *Truth, etc.* (Oxford: Oxford University Press, 2007). A very handy summary of basic logic principles without their history is found in Anthony Weston, *Rulebook for Arguments* (Indianapolis: Hackett, 2000).

For a general introduction to the philosophy of Plato and Aristotle see Roy Jackson, *Plato: A Beginner's Guide* (London: Hodder & Stoughton, 2001) and Rupert Woodfin, *Introducing Aristotle* (New York: Totem Books, 2006). A more detailed account of their epistemologies can be found in Richard Kraut, ed., *The Cambridge Companion to Plato* (Cambridge: Cambridge University Press, 1993) and J. Barnes, ed., *The Cambridge Companion to Aristotle* (Cambridge: Cambridge University Press, 1995).

Chapter 2

The passage called 'The Teacher Within' comes from Augustine's work, *De magistro,* in *Augustine: De magistro* and *De Libero Arbitrio*, ed. K. D. Daur and W. M. Green (Turnholt: Brepols, 1970), pp. 197–202. For an English translation of the entire work see Augustine, *Against the Academicians and the Teacher*, trans. Peter King (Indianapolis: Hackett, 1995).

The passage called 'God and Truth' comes from Augustine's work, *De Libero Arbitrio* in *Augustine: De magistro* and *De Libero Arbitro*, op. cit., pp. 260–4. For an English translation of the entire work see Augustine, *On Free Choice of the Will*, trans. Thomas Williams (Indianapolis: Hackett, 1993).

The passage called 'The Greatest Conceivable Being' comes from Anselm's *Proslogium*, chapter II, which can be found at the following site on the Internet: http://www.fordham.edu/halsall/basis/anselm-proslogium.html#CHAPTER%20II, Internet Medieval Sourcebook, ed. Paul Halsall. For an English translation of the entire work see *St. Anselm's Proslogion with A reply on behalf of the fool, by Gaunilo, and the author's reply to Gaunilo*, ed. M. J. Charlesworth (Oxford: Clarendon Press, 1965). The passage by Gaunilo called 'On Behalf of the Fool' is included in both of the above sources.

The passage called 'Against Anselm' comes from *Thomas Aquinas: Summa Theologica part I, question 2, article 1,* ed. The Blackfriars (New York: McGraw-Hill, 1964), vol. II, pp. 4–6. An English translation of the entire article can be found at the following site on the Internet: 'The *Summa Theologica* of St Thomas Aquinas,' trans. Fathers of the English Dominican Province, New Advent Online Edition, ed. Kevin Knight, http://www.newadvent.org/summa/1002.htm.

Augustine's *City of God* is available in English translation by Henry Bettenson (New York: Penguin Classics, 2003). For a general introduction to Augustine's philosophy see *The Cambridge Companion to Augustine,* ed. Eleonore Stump and Norman Kretzmann (Cambridge: Cambridge University Press, 2001).

Chapter 3

The passage called 'Unhappiness' comes from *Augustine: De Libero Arbitrio,* ed. W. M. Green (Turnholt: Brepols, 1970), pp. 289–91. For an English translation of the relevant section of the work see Augustine, *On Free Choice of the will,* trans. Thomas Williams (Indianapolis: Hackett, 1993), pp. 87–90.

The passage 'Evil Is Not a Thing' comes from *Enchiridion theologicum Sancti Augustini,* ed. Franciscus Moriones (Madrid: La Editorial Católica, 1961), pp. 10–12. For an English translation of the entire work see Augustine, *Enchiridion on Faith, Hope, and Love* (Washington DC: Gateway Editions, 1996).

The passage 'Free Will' comes from Fr. Petrus Iohannis Olivi, O.F.M., *Quaestiones in II librum Sententiarum* (Quaracchi: Collegii S. Bonaventurae, 1924), vol. II, Q. LVII, p. 369. It is not published in English translation.

For a general introduction to the problem of suffering see Richard Swinburne, *The Coherence of Theism* (Oxford: Clarendon Press, 1997). See also Robert Adams, 'Must God Create the Best?' in *The Virtue of Faith and Other Essays in Philosophical Theology* (New York: Oxford University Press), pp. 51–64, and Thomas Morris, 'Perfection and Creation,' in Eleonore Stump, ed., *Reasoned Faith* (Ithaca: Cornell University Press), pp. 234–47.

For a general introduction to the free will–determinism debate, see Ted Honderich, *How Free Are You?: The Determinism Problem* (New York: Oxford University Press, 2002) or Robert Kane, *A Contemporary Introduction to Free Will* (New York: Oxford University Press, 2005).

The news story about the severe case of child abuse came from an article called 'Worst Case of Child Abuse in Forty Years,' dated 11 December 2000 in the *Berkeley Daily Planet*, http://www. berkeleydaily.org.

Chapter 4

The passages called 'There Was No Time before Time' and 'The Nature of Time' come from *The Confessions of Saint Augustine*, ed. by J. J. O'Donnell, http://www.stoa.org/hippo/text11.html. For an English translation of this work see Augustine, *Confessions*, trans. H. Chadwick (Oxford: Oxford University Press, 1998). See also the following site on the Internet: 'Confessions,' trans. E. B. Pusey, http://ccat.sas.upenn.edu/jod/augustine/Pusey/book11.

The passages called 'The Conflict between Foreknowledge and Free Will' and 'Lady Philosophy's Answer' come from '*Boethius Consolatio Philosophae*,' ed. G. Weinberger (Vienna, 1935, volume 67 in the series Corpus Scriptorum Ecclesiasticorum Latinorum), http://ccat.sas.upenn.edu/jod/boethius/jkok/list_t.htm. For an English translation of the entire work see Boethius, *The Consolation of Philosophy*, trans. V. Watts (Harmondsworth: Penguin Classics, 2000). See also *The Consolation of Philosophy by Boethius*, trans. W. V. Cooper (J. M. Dent and Company: London, 1902), available at the following site on the Internet: Electronic Text Center: University of Virginia Library http://ccat.sas.upenn.edu/jod/boethius/boetrans.html.

The passage called 'God Is beyond Our Understanding' comes from *Meister Eckhart: Die deutschen und lateinischen Werke* (Stuttgart and Berlin: W. Kohlhammer, 1936), ch. 20, section 174ff. For an English translation of the relevant section see Meister Eckhart, 'Commentary on Exodus,' trans. Bernard McGinn in *Meister Eckhart, Teacher and Preacher* (New York: Paulist Press, 1987), pp. 98–9.

For a general introduction to the issues covered in this chapter see William Lane Craig, *Time and Eternity: Exploring God's Relationship to*

Time (Wheaton, ILL.: Crossway Books, 2001). For an examination of Augustine's view of these issues see Charlotte Gross, 'Augustine's Ambivalence about Temporality: His Two Accounts of Time,' *Medieval Philosophy and Theology* 8.2 (1999), pp. 129–48, along with Katherine A. Rogers, 'St Augustine on Time and Eternity,' *American Catholic Philosophical Quarterly* 70.2 (1996), pp. 207–23. Finally, Murry Macbeath provides some interesting insights into the issue in 'Omniscience and Eternity,' *Aristotelian Society: Supplementary Volume*, SUPP 63 (1989), pp. 55–73.

Chapter 5

The passage 'There Must Have Been a Beginning' comes from *Thomas Aquinas: Summa Theologica part I, question 2, article 3*, ed. The Blackfriars (New York: McGraw-Hill, 1964), vol. II, pp. 12–14. For an English translation of the entire article see 'The *Summa Theologica* of St Thomas Aquinas,' trans. Fathers of the English Dominican Province, New Advent Online Edition, ed. Kevin Knight, http://www.newadvent. org/summa/1002.htm. Aquinas actually adopts an agnostic view along the lines of Maimonides in a different work on this issue. See Ralph McInerny's translation of Thomas Aquinas's 'On the Eternity of the World against Murmurers,' in *A First Glance at St. Thomas Aquinas: A Handbook for Peeping Thomists* (Notre Dame: University of Notre Dame Press, 1990), pp. 49–56.

The passage 'There Was No Beginning' comes from Averroes, '*Destructio destructionum philosophiae Algazelis,' in the Latin version of Calo Calonymos*, ed. Beatrice H. Zedler (Milwaukee: Marquette University Press, 1961), pp. 79–82. For an English translation of the relevant text see *Tahafut al-Tahafut*, trans. Simon Van Den Bergh (London: Luzac & Co., 1969), pp. 9–14. See also the following site by the same translator on the Internet: http://www.muslimphilosophy.com/ir/tt/tt-ch1. htm#p1.

For an overview of the Arabic contribution to this issue see William Lane Craig, *The Kalam Cosmological Argument* (Eugene, OR: Wipf & Stock Publishers, 2000). This is a reprint of William Lane Craig's 1979 book by the same name which has been widely discussed ever since. It is divided into two main sections. The first is about the history of the arguments. The second is a modern defence of it, including both philosophical and scientific arguments for the finitude of the past.

The passage 'It Can't Be Determined' comes from Moshe ben Maymon, *Rabi Mossei Aegyptii Dux seu director dubitatium aut perplexorum: in tres libros* (Parrhisiis: Ab Iocodo Badio Ascensio, 1520), pt 2, ch. 17. For an English translation of the entire work see Maimonides, *The Guide for the Perplexed*, trans. M. Friedlander (New York: Dover, 1956). For a general introduction to Maimonides on this issue see Kenneth Seeskin, *Maimonides on the Origin of the World* (New York: Cambridge University Press, 2005).

The thought experiment about the infinite number of cars is based on a thought experiment called 'Hilbert's Hotel,' originally proposed by David Hilbert (1862–1943). There is an intriguing nine-minute film about it called 'Hotel Infinity,' dir. Amanda Boyle (London: Picture Farm, 2004).

There is an informative twenty-minute film about contemporary theories of the age of the universe called 'The Expanding Universe: From Big Bang to Big Crunch?' *The Complete Cosmos* (Princeton, NJ: Films for the Humanities and Sciences, 1998).

For a more detailed examination of the medieval debate on the topic covered in this chapter see R. C. Dales, *Medieval Discussions of the Eternity of the World* (Leiden: Brill, 1990). It presents and discusses a number of medieval authors and provides an extensive bibliographic guide.

Chapter 6

For a complete translation of Empedocles's fragments see Kathleen Freeman, *Ancilla to the Pre-Socratic Philosophers* (Cambridge: Harvard University Press, 1966), pp. 51–64. For a reconstruction from fragments and secondary sources see D. O'Brien, *Empedocles' Cosmic Cycle* (Cambridge: Cambridge University Press, 1969). For a compelling interpretation of Empedocles with English translation see Edwin L. Minar, Jr, 'Cosmic Periods in the Philosophy of Empedocles,' *Phronesis* 8 (1963), pp. 127–45.

The passage called 'Empedocles's Explanation' comes from *Aristotle: Physics*, ed. Philip H. Wicksteed and Francis M. Cornford, vol. II (New York: G. P. Putnam's Sons, 1929–34), pp. 169–73. For an English translation see *Physics*, book II, trans. R. P. Hardie and R. K. Gaye in *The Basic Works of Aristotle*, edited by Richard McKeon (New York: Random House, 1941), p. 249. See also the following site on the Internet: *Physics, by Aristotle*, translated by R. P. Hardie and R. K. Gaye, Internet Classics Archive, http://classics.mit.edu/Aristotle/physics.2.ii.html.

The passage called 'There is Purpose in Nature' comes from *Thomas Aquinas: Summa Theologica part I, question 2, article 3*, ed. The Blackfriars (New York: McGraw-Hill, 1964), vol. II, p. 16. For an English translation of the entire article see 'The *Summa Theologica* of St. Thomas Aquinas,' trans. Fathers of the English Dominican Province, New Advent Online Edition, ed. Kevin Knight, http://www.newadvent.org/summa/1002.htm.

The passage called 'Purpose Is Not Observable' is an amalgam of two separate works of William of Ockham. The first is Quodlibet 4, question 1. It comes from Guillelmi de Ockham, *Opera Theologica*, Gedeon Gál *et al.*, eds. (St Bonaventure, NY: Franciscan Institute, 1967–86), vol. IX, pp. 295–9. For an English translation of the entire question see William of Ockham, *Quodlibetal Questions, quod. IV, question 35,* trans. Alfred J. Freddoso and Francis E. Kelley (New Haven: Yale University Press, 1991), pp. 246–9. The second work is Ockham's Commentary on Aristotle's *Physics*. It comes from Guillelmi de Ockham, *Opera Philosophica*, Gedeon Gál *et al.,* eds. (St Bonaventure, NY: Franciscan Institute, 1967–86), vol. IV, pp. 370–4. This work is not published in English translation.

The passage called 'The Simplicity Objection' comes from *Thomas Aquinas: Summa Theologica part I, question 2, article 3,* ed. The Blackfriars (New York: McGraw-Hill, 1977), vol. II, pp. 12–16. For an English translation of the entire article see 'The *Summa Theologica* of St. Thomas Aquinas,' trans. Fathers of the English Dominican Province, New Advent Online Edition, ed. Kevin Knight, http://www.newadvent.org/summa/1002.htm.

Chatton's Anti-Razor is found in his *Lectura* I d.3 q 1, a. 1, which is unpublished. For the relevant texts and discussion see Armand Maurer, 'Ockham's Razor and Chatton's Anti-Razor,' *Medieval Studies* 46 (1984), pp. 463–75.

For a more detailed account of Aquinas's arguments for the existence of God see D. Bonnette, *Aquinas' Proofs for God's Existence: St Thomas Aquinas on 'the Per Accidens necessarily implies the Per Se'* (Springer, 2002). For a more detailed account of Ockham's view of nature as well as his use of the principle of simplicity see M. M. Adams, William Ockham (Notre Dame: Notre Dame UP, 1989).

The example about the nativity scene etched in the frost on the window comes from Robert Hamburger, 'The Argument from Design,' in *Intention and Intentionality*, ed. Cora Diamond (Ithaca: Cornell University Press): pp. 109–31.

For an introduction to the controversy surrounding the anthropic principle see John D. Barrow and Frank J. Tipler, *The Anthropic Cosmological Principle* (New York: Oxford University Press, 1986).

For a modern critique of teleology from the point of view of a scientist see Richard Dawkins, *The Blind Watchmaker: Why the Evidence of Evolution Reveals a Universe Without Design* (New York: W. W. Norton & Company, 1996). It was originally published in 1986, winning the Royal Society of Literature's Heinemann Prize and the Los Angeles Times Book Award. See also Dawkins's more recent work, *The God Delusion* (New York: Houghton Mifflin, 2006). For a modern critique of teleology from the point of view of a philosopher see Daniel C. Dennett, *Darwin's Dangerous Idea: Evolution and the Meanings of Life* (New York: Simon & Schuster 1995).

For the modern defence of teleology see William A. Dembski, *Intelligent Design: The Bridge Between Science & Theology* (Intervarsity Press: ILL, 2002) and Thomas Woodward, *Darwin Strikes Back: Defending the Science of Intelligent Design* (Dartmouth, MA: Baker Books, 2006). For a debate featuring prominent representatives of both sides of the issue see Robert M. Baird and Stuart E. Rosenbaum, eds., *Intelligent Design: Real Science or Religion in Disguise* (New York: Prometheus Books, 2007).

The seven-part video production *Evolution* (WGBH/NOVA Science Unit and Clear Blue Sky Productions, 2001) provides an excellent introduction to the concept of evolution by natural selection along with the controversies it has sparked. Part five, 'Why Sex?' is especially interesting because it shows how evolution by natural selection can provide a purely biological account of human love and romance.

Chapter 7

The passage 'Critique of Immanent Realism' comes from Abelard's *Logica Ingredientibus*, in '*Peter Abaelards Philosophische Schriften*,' ed. B. Geyer in *Beitrage zur Geschichte der Philosophie des Mittelalters*, bd. xxi, (Munster I. W., 1919), p. 9. For an English translation of the relevant section of this work see Abelard, 'The Existence and the Nature of Universals,' trans. M. M. Tweedale, in *Basic Issues in Medieval Philosophy*, ed. Richard N. Bosley and Martin Tweedale (Peterborough, CA: Broadview, 1996), pp. 378–92.

The passage called 'The Logic of Universal Nouns' comes from Abelard's *Logica Petitiorum Sociorum*, in '*Peter Abaelards Philosophische Schriften*,' op. cit., pp. 530–3. For an English translation of the relevant section of this work see Abelard, 'Universals and Signification,' trans. M. M. Tweedale, in *Basic Issues in Medieval Philosophy*, ed. Richard N. Bosley and Martin Tweedale (Peterborough, CA: Broadview, 1996), pp. 392–4.

The passage 'Metaphysical Unity' comes from Ioannis Duns Scoti, *Ordinatio II, dist. iii, pt.1, q.1* in *Opera Omnia*, vol. VII, ed. P. C. Balic (Vatican: Typis Polyglottis Vaticanis, 1973), p. 399. For an English translation of the relevant section of this work see John Duns Scotus, 'Natures Are Not of Themselves Individuated,' trans. M. M. Tweedale, in *Basic Issues in Medieval Philosophy*, ed. Richard N. Bosley and Martin Tweedale (Peterborough, CA: Broadview, 1996), pp. 404–10.

The passage 'Against Scotus and Abelard' is an amalgam of two separate works of Ockham. The first is Quodlibet IV, question 35. It comes from Guillelmi de Ockham, *Opera Theologica*, Gedeon Gál *et al.,* eds. (St. Bonaventure, NY: Franciscan Institute, 1967–86), vol. IX, pp. 472–4. For an English translation of the entire quodlibet see William of Ockham, *Quodlibetal Questions, quod. IV, question 35,* trans. Alfred J. Freddoso and Francis E. Kelley (New Haven: Yale University Press, 1991), pp. 387–91. The second work is *Summa Logicae,* part 1, ch. 51. It comes from Guillelmi de Ockham, *Opera Philosophica*, Gedeon Gál *et al.,* eds. (St Bonaventure, NY: Franciscan Institute, 1967–86), vol. I, pp. 472–4. For an English translation of this work see *Ockham's Theory of Terms: Part One of the Summa Logicae*, trans. Michael J. Loux (Notre Dame: University of Notre Dame Press, 1974), p. 169.

For a general introduction to the topic covered in this chapter see
J. Gracia's two volumes: *Introduction to the Problem of Individuation in the
Early Middle Ages* (Washington, DC: Catholic University of America
Press, 1984) and *Individuation in Scholasticism: The Later Middle Ages and
the Counter Reformation (1150–1650)*, (Albany, NY: SUNY Press,
1994). For a more detailed study of Abelard's account, see Martin
Tweedale, *Abailard on Universals* (Amsterdam: North-Holland, 1976).
For a more detailed study of Scotus see Richard Cross, *Duns Scotus*
(Oxford: Oxford University Press, 1999). For a more detailed study of
Ockham see M. M. Adams, *William Ockham* (Notre Dame: University
of Notre Dame Press, 1989).

Chapter 8

The passage called 'Natural Law' comes from *Thomas Aquinas: Summa
Theologica part I-II, question 94*, ed. The Blackfriars (New York:
McGraw-Hill, 1966), vol. XXVIII, pp. 78–83. For an English transla-
tion of the entire article see 'The *Summa Theologica* of St Thomas
Aquinas,' trans. Fathers of the English Dominican Province, New
Advent Online Edition, ed. Kevin Knight, http://www.newadvent.
org/summa/1002.htm.

The passage called 'On Drunkenness' comes from *Thomas Aquinas:
Summa Theologica part II-II, question 150*, ed. The Blackfriars (New
York: McGraw-Hill, 1964), vol. XLIII, p. 148. For an English transla-
tion of the entire article see 'The *Summa Theologica* of St. Thomas
Aquinas,' trans. Fathers of the English Dominican Province, New
Advent Online Edition, ed. Kevin Knight, http://www.newadvent.
org/summa/3150.htm

The passage called 'Right and Wrong Are Not Universals' is an
amalgam of two separate sections of Ockham's *Reportatio*. They come
from Guillelmi de Ockham, *Opera Theologica*, Gedeon Gál *et al.*, eds.
(St Bonaventure, NY: Franciscan Institute, 1967–86), vol. V, p. 352,
and vol. VII, pp. 195–8, respectively. This work is not published in
English translation.

The passage called 'The Best Person and the Best Laws' comes from
Jacobi de Viterbo, O. E. S. A. Quod. IV, question 30 in *Disputatio
quarta de quolibet,* edited by Eelcko Ypma (Würzburg: Augustinus-

Verlag, 1975). For an English translation of the entire question see *The Cambridge Translations of Medieval Philosophical Texts,* vol. II, ed. A. S. Mcgrade *et al.* (Cambridge: Cambridge University Press, 2001), pp. 324–5.

For a general introduction to Aquinas's natural law theory see Anthony J. Lisska, *Aquinas's Theory of Natural Law: An Analytic Reconstruction* (New York: Oxford University Press, 2002). For a general introduction to Ockham's divine command ethics see Lucan Freppert, *The Basis of Morality according to William Ockham* (Chicago: Franciscan Herald Press, 1988). For general background to medieval ethics as well as other topics covered in this book see *The Cambridge Companion to Medieval Philosophy*, ed. A. S. McGrade (Cambridge: Cambridge University Press, 2003).

Index